Writing across the curriculum

Year 5

Jonathan Rooke and Stacey Collins

Jonathan Rooke is a senior lecturer at University College, Winchester. He worked as a primary school teacher before becoming a literacy consulant. He has written for various professional publications and co-authored 'Creativity and Writing Skills' with Kay Hiatt.

Stacey Collins is an experienced teacher who is currently teaching Year 6 children in Alton, Hampshire. She has been curriculum manager of literacy for four years. In 2002, she became one of Hampshire's 'Leading Literacy' teachers, carrying out developmental projects and research in school.

Contents

Published by
Hopscotch Educational Publishing Ltd
Unit 2
The Old Brushworks
56 Pickwick Road
Corsham
Wiltshire
SN13 9BX

01249 701701

© 2004 Hopscotch Educational Publishing

Written by Jonathan Rooke and Stacey Collins
Series design by Blade Communications
Cover illustration by Susan Hutchison
Illustrated by Jean de Lemos
Printed by Colorman (Ireland) Ltd

ISBN 1-904307-36-1

Jonathan Rooke and Stacey Collins hereby assert their moral right to be identified as the authors of this work in accordance with the Copyright, Designs and Patents Act, 1988.

Every effort has been made to trace the owners of copyright of material in this book and the publisher apologises for any inadvertent omissions. Any persons claiming copyright for any material should contact the publisher who will be happy to pay the permission fees agreed between them and who will amend the information in this book on any subsequent reprint.

The text on page 71 is taken from *Ancient Greek Myths and Legends* by Philip Ardagh, published by Belitha Press. ISBN 1-85561-725-0

The layout on page 85 is taken from *First Steps*, published by Rigby Heinemann (formerly Heinemann Ginn Professional Publishing), 1999

Introduction

About the series

Writing Across the Curriculum is a series of books aimed at developing and enriching the writing skills of children at Key Stage 2. Matched to the National Literacy Strategy's *Framework for Teaching* and the QCA's Schemes of Work, each book contains comprehensive lesson plans in two different subject areas for recount, report, instruction, explanation, persuasion and discussion (in Year 6) writing.

There are four books in the series: Year 3, Year 4, Year 5 and Year 6.

Each book aims to:

- support teachers by providing detailed lesson plans on how to incorporate the teaching of writing skills within different subject areas;

- develop teachers' confidence in using modelled writing sessions by providing example scripts that the teachers can use or adapt;

- reduce teachers' preparation time through the provision of photocopiable resources;

- develop and enhance children's writing skills through stimulating and purposeful activities;

- encourage children's enjoyment of writing.

About each book

Each book is divided into separate chapters for each writing genre. Each chapter contains:

- an introductory page of teachers' notes that outlines the key structural and linguistic features and guidelines on the teaching and progression of that particular writing genre;

- two units of work, each on a different subject area.

Each unit of work is divided into four lesson plans that can be carried out over a period of time. These lessons are called:

'Switching on' – introduces the concepts;

'Revving up' – develops the concepts;

'Taking off' – instigates the planning stage of the writing;

'Flying solo' – encourages independent writing.

Each lesson plan is divided as follows:

- Learning objectives;

- Resources;

- What to do;

- Plenary.

Most lessons are supported by **photocopiable sheets**. Some of these sheets provide background information for the children and others provide support in the form of writing frames. Most lessons have an exemplar text that can be shared with the children. There is usually an annotated version of this text for the teacher. The annotated version points out the structural and linguistic features of the text. It should be noted, however, that only one example of each feature is provided and that the features are presented as a guide only.

Recount writing

What is a recount text?

A recount is quite simply a retelling of an event. The retelling can be used to impart information or to entertain the reader. Recounts can be personal (from the point of view of someone who was there) or impersonal.

Structural features

- Usually begins with an introduction to orientate the reader. Often answers the questions 'who?', 'what?', 'when?', 'where?' and 'why?'
- Main body of text then retells the events in chronological order
- Ends with a conclusion that briefly summarises the text or comments on the event

Linguistic features

- Past tense
- First person (personal recounts) or third person (impersonal)
- Focuses on named individuals or participants
- Use of time connectives to aid chronological order (firstly, afterwards, meanwhile, subsequently, finally)
- Often contains interesting details to bring incidents alive to the reader

Examples of recount texts

- newspaper reports
- diary entries
- letters
- write-up of trips or activities
- autobiographies/biographies

Teaching recount writing

At first glance, recounts seem to be relatively straightforward; after all, children seem to get plenty of practice doing their 'news' writing at school! However, as with any retelling, it is easy for children to neglect to include vital pieces of information. The knowledge of the event is in the children's heads and it is our job, as teachers, to make sure that that knowledge is shared with the reader in order to make the event purposeful for them. Children tend to list events, as if on a timeline, but they need to include specific information and use relevant connectives so that the reader is able to have all the information needed to imagine themselves there.

Many children need a lot of support in organising the information chronologically. A flow chart is a useful tool to enable children to sequence events in the correct order. It also enables them to see where there are natural divisions for paragraphs. A word bank of time connectives could also prove useful.

Encourage the children to organise the planning of their recount by listing information under the headings: who, what, when, where and why. This will ensure they include all the vital information.

Recount writing – progression

Simple recounts are introduced in Key Stage 1 (Reception – T15; Year 1 – Term 3: T20).

In Year 3 children experiment with recounting the same event in a variety of ways, such as a story, a letter or a newspaper report (Term 3: T22).

In Year 4 children examine opening sentences that set scenes and capture interest and identify the key features of newspapers (Term 1: T18, T20). They write newspaper-style reports (Term 1: T24). They learn to make short notes (Term 2: T21).

In **Year 5** (Term 1: T21, T23, T24, T26) children learn to identify the features of recounted texts such as sports reports and diaries and to write recounts based on subject, topic or personal experiences for different audiences. They discuss the purpose of note taking and how this influences the nature of the notes made.

In Year 6 (Term 1: T11, T14, T15, T16; Term 3: T19, T22) children are reading to distinguish between biography and autobiography and are developing the skills of biographical and autobiographical writing in role. They review a range of text features and select the appropriate style and form to suit a specific purpose and audience.

Unit 1

Lesson focus

Physical Education Unit 3 – Invasion games

Overall aim

To write a recount of an invasion game in the style of a sports report.

Physical Education emphasis

This unit builds on the children's knowledge and understanding of invasion games and develops their skills, focusing on strategies and tactics within games. The children are required to play small sided games and evaluate performance in terms of tactics, suggesting appropriate strategies for improvement.

Writing a sports report will help children develop the skills needed to observe, reflect and comment critically on a game/match within a clear structure and framework of a recount text.

Literacy links

Year 5, Term 1: T21, T24

About this unit

This unit is suitable for use within literacy time over four days/one week or can be split between literacy and PE time. How you choose to deliver it will depend upon your class and time restrictions within the curriculum but it is best taught as a continuous unit over one week. As part of PE the children should have learned and played invasion games so that they are able to play and observe small sided games effectively before writing. It may be useful for them to collect sports reports from newspapers and magazines to help with the identification of features.

Switching on

Learning objectives

- To be able to identify the key features of news reports and journalistic writing.
- To understand how sports reports use expressive language and elaboration.

Resources

- Sheets A, B and C (pages 9 to 11)

What to do

Explain to the children that in the next few lessons they will be looking at sports reports in order to write their own. Where are sports reports usually found? What is their purpose? What do they know about how these are written? (Some children may suggest past tense, retelling and so on – list their responses.) Tell them that they will be writing their own sports reports about a game that they have played, but they need to learn about the special features of a sports report first. Explain that a sports report is a recount because it is a retelling of an event that has already happened.

Share an enlarged version of Sheet B. Read through the text together; what are the children's initial responses? Does it sound like an exciting game? Why/why not?

Now share an enlarged version of Sheet C. Explain to the children that this is a different report of the same game. What are their responses this time? Which report do they prefer/think is most effective? Why? What are the differences/similarities in the two reports? (They include the same facts but the language used is different.)

Using Sheet A as your guide, draw out the key structural and linguistic features of the texts and annotate them on the larger versions of Sheets B and C. Pay particular attention to the use of expressive language and elaboration. For example, the use of the words 'thunderous', 'magnificent', 'determined' and 'stunning' on Sheet C.

Plenary

Ask the children to tell you what they have learned about the features of a sports report. Together, create a simple checklist of features that can be kept and used as a reference in later lessons.

Revving up

Learning objectives

■ To be able to identify the key events in a game.

■ To begin to write a sports report, using notes.

Resources

■ Sheets D, E and F (pages 12 to 14)

What to do

Tell the children that you have borrowed some notes from a journalist. Share an enlarged version of Sheet D. Explain that you will be using these notes to write a report of the game. Ask them what problems you might have. (Because you haven't seen the game you will have to rely on the accuracy of the notes.)

Use a blank OHT or flip chart to model writing the report; you can use the following notes to 'cheat' but make sure that you talk to the children as you write, describing what you are doing and explaining your language choices. Refer to the checklist made in the 'Switching on' session and let the children make suggestions where appropriate.

The following is a suggestion for a text to use when modelling writing. The children should not see the text but think that you are really making it up as you go along. The idea is that you show the children how to write while explaining your thinking at the same time.

The bold print is what you actually write and the italics can be used as a script of what to say to the children.

Okay, so I'm going to have a go at writing a recount of the game between Nowin United and Goalless City. I didn't see the game but I can use the notes on Sheet D. First of all I need an opening paragraph – what am I writing about?… **On 12th December…** *I must remember to use the past tense because it has already happened…* **Nowin United played** *(past tense)* **Goalless City at the Nohope Ground.** *Well, that's it but I think I'd like to add a little bit more – I'll use the notes in section 4.* **Both teams had experienced disappointing seasons and Nowin were without their star goal scorer, Kevin Kickman.**

That will do; now I need to go into what happened in time order. I can use opinions and must remember to use proper nouns. **The first** *(indicates time)* **14 minutes of the game were uneventful.** *The notes don't give any information until the 15th minute.* **In the 15th minute Bertie Boot, of Nowin Utd, was given a yellow card for a late tackle against City's Stanley Striker.** *I want to mention now that no one scored and that it was a bit of a boring game as I can see in section 7 of the notes on Sheet D.* **Striker later** *(time connective)* **took a free kick but this was saved by Nowin's goalie, Charlie Keeper, who just happened to be in the right place at the right time. Still** *(time connective)* **with no goals by half-time the fans were getting restless.**

New paragraph to go on to second half – I need to try and use some more powerful or descriptive words. **As** *(here I am using a time connective)* **the players resumed play after** *(another time connective)* **half-time they appeared tired and listless. During** *(another time connective)* **play both teams lacked concentration and struggled to keep possession of the ball.** *I think I'll mention the fans again to emphasise how dull the game was.* **Fans looked on as their teams bumbled around the pitch. Some got up and left, furious that they had wasted their money on such a dreadful game. The fans had to wait until** *(another time connective)* **the 69th minute for another glimpse of some action. Steve Slider's late tackle on Nowin's striker, Usef Upfront, gave Nowin a chance at goal. Seconds later,** *(another time connective)* **Upfront's penalty shot was stopped with a superb save** *(alliteration)* **by City's goalie, Hans Missing.** *Right, now I need to do a closing statement to end the recount.*

Final paragraph – I need to recap and give the outcome as well as mention the replay. **After** *(another time connective)* **a disappointing game the final score was a 0 – 0 draw. The two teams will meet again** (another time connective) **for a replay later** (another time connective) **in the season.** Opinion… **Let's hope that both teams pick up their game as the battle** (strong word to indicate competition) **for promotion continues.**

Now let's reread it and see if we can improve or alter any parts. Have I used the features accurately?

When you have finished, read through your report with the children. Do they think you have included all the features of a sports report? Can they suggest any improvements?

Provide the children with another set of notes (Sheet E or some of your own). Explain that they are now going to use these notes to write a sports report in the same way as you have just done. Remind them to refer to the checklist of features made in 'Switching on'. (Less able children could use the notes to produce a comic strip (Sheet F) showing the game.) Depending on the dynamics of your class it may be helpful for the children to work in pairs to write their reports.

Plenary

When the children have finished writing, they should swap their reports with another child/pair. They can then read each other's reports and evaluate them against the checklist. Ask them to express their opinions about the effectiveness of the report and give positive suggestions for improvement.

Taking off

Learning objectives

■ To be able to play a small sided game using skills and tactics as part of a team.

■ To make notes.

Resources

■ Sheet G (page 15)

■ Area suitable for PE

■ Video camera (optional)

What to do

This is a very active lesson! Explain to the children that they will take it in turns to play a game and to make notes while they watch. Remind them of the important information they will need to record when watching. You may choose to provide them with a copy of Sheet G to use as a prompt.

Split the class into two sets of three teams and set up small sided games of your choice (these should be invasion games such as football, rugby, netball or hockey). At any one time there will be four teams playing and two teams observing, as follows:

Teams A, B, C	Teams D, E, F
A v B (C observe)	D v E (F observe)
B v C (A observe)	E v F (D observe)
C v A (B observe)	F v D (E observe)

This means that each child will take notes for one game. Allow a set time for each game (for example, five minutes).

Back in class let the children have time to look over and compare their notes (it is acceptable for them to add extra information at this point if they feel someone else has important information that they did not record themselves).

Plenary

After a few minutes, choose one or two children to give an oral retelling of the game using their notes to help them. How easy/difficult is it? What improvements would they need to make if they did this in writing? Ask the children to give their responses and encourage them to explain/give reasons for their opinions by referring to the checklist.

Flying solo

Learning objectives

■ To identify the key events within an invasion game and report on the scoring and possession.
■ To write a sports report.

Resources

■ Sheet C (page 11) and Sheet H (page 16)
■ Notes from the 'Taking off' session

What to do

Remind the children of the notes made in the previous lesson. Explain that they will be using their notes to write their own sports report (recount). How confident are they that their notes will be helpful to them? Do they think they need to make any alterations/additions?

Ask them to remind you about the special features of sports reports. Show them the checklist and remind them that they will be expected to use these features in their own writing.

Share an enlarged version of Sheet C. Look at the structure and ask the children: 'How is it organised? How does it start and finish? What type of language is used?' Make a list of useful connectives (see page 4 for some suggestions).

Ask the children to suggest opening sentences and begin to model writing the first paragraph. Now they should be ready to work independently to write their own reports. Less able children may need a copy of Sheet H to help them. Support them as they write, reminding them of the features they should be using.

Plenary

Bring the class back together. How do they feel about the piece of writing they have done? Did they use all the features? Have they made it interesting by using expressive language? If possible put one or two examples onto OHTs to share with the rest of the class. Ask the children to evaluate the writing against the checklist and make positive suggestions for improvement.

Writing across the Curriculum

opening to set the scene and orientate the reader

use of specific names and proper nouns

Kicking Wanderers v Dribble Rovers

Fans watched as Kicking Wanderers beat Dribble Rovers at Old Scaffold last night.

The game got off to a slow start with the score being 0 – 0 at half-time. After 45 minutes on the pitch neither team had managed to score, despite several attempts by both sides. Just before the half-time whistle Striker Boots had a shot at the goal but the ball was saved by Rovers' keeper.

time connective

Following the half-time interval, fans watched as the teams returned to play. It seemed as though they were watching a different game, with both sides picking up the pace and trying to keep greater possession of the ball.

connective

Before long Gary Goaler scored a goal to take Wanderers into a 1 – 0 lead in the 69th minute. Minutes later Boots followed this up with a long shot that hit the target to make it 2 – 0 after 75 minutes.

personal opinion/ observational comment

detailed information

With Kicking Wanderers 2 – 0 up, Dribble Rovers played a defensive game for the remaining 15 minutes. Meanwhile, Wanderers kept up attempts at goal but without success.

At full time the score was 2 – 0 to Kicking Wanderers. Dribble Rovers have not won at Old Scaffold for eight years.

events recounted in chronological order

conclusion/ closing statement

Kicking Wanderers Fight Back

After a disappointing start to the season, Kicking Wanderers were back on track last night as they fought their way to a 2 – 0 victory over Dribble Rovers.

opening to set the scene and orientate the reader

It really was a game of two halves yesterday as fans saw little action in the first half. During the first 45 minutes of play the only real shot at goal was made by Striker Boots. This thunderous shot was met with a magnificent save by Rovers' keeper.

powerful adjectives to create dramatic effect

At the end of the first half the score at Old Scaffold was 0 – 0 and fans were left feeling disappointed.

At half-time both teams evidently received heated team talks from their managers; the two teams who walked back onto the pitch were unrecognisable from the first half. Dribble Rovers picked up the pace and made several attempts at goal. Meanwhile, Kicking Wanderers were fired up and determined to fight back.

writer's opinion

Prior to either team scoring, two players were shown the yellow card. Before long, Gary Goaler drilled the ball into the back of the net to take Wanderers into the lead, 1 – 0 after 69 minutes. Fans didn't have to wait too long for the next goal in this action packed game: within minutes Striker Boots smashed a stunning second goal into the back of the net. With the score at 2 – 0 after 75 minutes Rovers returned to a defensive game. Meanwhile, Wanderers kept up the pace to maintain their 2 goal lead.

conclusion/ closing statement

Dribble Rovers have not won at Old Scaffold for eight years and their hopes were killed off by Boots last night. The England star and defender Goaler secured their team's third place position in the premiership.

alliteration

Kicking Wanderers v Dribble Rovers.

Fans watched as Kicking Wanderers beat Dribble Rovers at Old Scaffold last night.

The game got off to a slow start with the score being 0 – 0 at half-time. After 45 minutes on the pitch neither team had managed to score, despite several attempts by both sides. Just before the half-time whistle Striker Boots had a shot at the goal but the ball was saved by Rovers' keeper.

A superb save from Rovers' keeper

Following the half-time interval, fans watched as the teams returned to play. It seemed as though they were watching a different game, with both sides picking up the pace and trying to keep greater possession of the ball.

Before long Gary Goaler scored a goal to take Wanderers into a 1 – 0 lead in the 69th minute. Minutes later Boots followed this up with a long shot that hit the target to make it 2 – 0 after 75 minutes.

Gary Goaler's superb goal curves around the keeper

With Kicking Wanderers 2 – 0 up, Dribble Rovers played a defensive game for the remaining 15 minutes. Meanwhile, Wanderers kept up attempts at goal but without success.

At full time the score was 2 – 0 to Kicking Wanderers. Dribble Rovers have not won at Old Scaffold for eight years.

Kicking Wanderers Fight Back

A superb save from Rovers' keeper

After a disappointing start to the season, Kicking Wanderers were back on track last night as they fought their way to a 2 – 0 victory over Dribble Rovers.

It really was a game of two halves yesterday as fans saw little action in the first half. During the first 45 minutes of play the only real shot at goal was made by Striker Boots. This thunderous shot was met with a magnificent save by Rovers' keeper.

At the end of the first half the score at Old Scaffold was 0 – 0 and fans were left feeling disappointed.

At halftime both teams evidently received heated team talks from their managers; the two teams who walked back onto the pitch were unrecognisable from the first half. Dribble Rovers picked up the pace and made several attempts at goal. Meanwhile, Kicking Wanderers were fired up and determined to fight back.

Prior to either team scoring, two players were shown the yellow card. Before long, Gary Goaler drilled the ball into the back of the net to take Wanderers into the lead, 1 – 0 after 69 minutes. Fans didn't have to wait too long for the next goal in this action packed game: within minutes Striker Boots smashed a stunning second goal into the back of the net. With the score at 2 – 0 after 75 minutes Rovers returned to a defensive game. Meanwhile, Wanderers kept up the pace to maintain their 2 goal lead.

Gary Goaler drills the ball into the net.

Dribble Rovers have not won at Old Scaffold for 8 years and their hopes were killed off by Boots last night. The England star and defender Goaler secured their team's third place position in the premiership.

Notes of a game

1. Teams:

Nowin United v Goalless City

2. Venue:

Nohope Ground

3. Time/Date:

12th December (you may want to insert your own date)

4. Pre-match comments:

Both teams have had poor seasons so far.

Nowin's top scorer, Kevin Kickman, is injured and cannot play.

City's goalie, Hans Missing, will play but is sporting a sprained ankle.

A well matched game – cannot predict outcome.

5. Record of events:

a) <u>What happened</u>	b) <u>When</u>	c) <u>Who was involved</u>
Late tackle by Nowin Utd, yellow card given	15 minutes	Bertie Boot (NU) against Stanley Striker (GC)
Free kick by Goalless City	31 minutes	Stanley Striker (GC), saved by Charlie Keeper (NU)
Penalty given to Nowin	69 minutes	Usef Upfront (NU) tackled late by Steve Slider (GC)
Penalty saved	70 minutes	Usef Upfront's shot (NU) saved by goalie Hans Missing (GC)

6. Outcome:

0 – 0 draw

7. Post-match comments:

After half-time both teams seemed tired; some action from Nowin Utd following dirty sliding tackle from Slider.

Hans Missing made an excellent save to keep the score 0 – 0.

Both teams struggled to keep possession of the ball.

Replay later in season.

Notes of a game

1. Teams:
Goalless City v Nowin United

2. Venue:
Last Chance Stadium

3. Time/Date:
1st April

4. Pre-match comments:
Rematch following last game's disappointing no score draw. Both teams have been training hard and Nowin have appointed a new manager, Harold Highhopes, in an attempt to improve their luck. Both teams have a fully fit squad; Nowin's striker, Kevin Kickman, returns after his injury. Goalless have shown impressive form; their victory over Walking Wanderers was well deserved. Both teams have everything to play for as the winners will be promoted into the second division.

5. Record of events:

a) <u>What happened</u>	b) <u>When</u>	c) <u>Who was involved</u>
Goal attempted by Nowin	5 minutes	Kevin Kickman's header (NU) was on target but was skilfully saved by Hans Missing (GC)
Goalless take possession; Nowin defenders left standing	12 minutes	Steve Slider (GC) covered the length of the pitch, only to hit the post
Goal! Nowin into 1 – 0 lead	34 minutes	Kevin Kickman (NU) curled the ball beautifully into the back of the net
Penalty saved	50 minutes	Usef Upfront's shot (NU)
Half-time = 1 – 0 to Nowin		
Goal! Goalless make it 1 – 1	59 minutes	Stanley Striker's goal (GC) set up by team-mate Tommy Tackle; NU goalie, Keeper, dived in the wrong direction
Charlie		
Full time = 1 – 1	90 minutes	
Injury time	5 mins extra	
Goal! 2 – 1 to Nowin	1 minute left to go	Martin Midfield (GC) allowed Danny Driver (NU) a shot at goal; keeper Hans Missing (GC) wasn't quick enough to save it

6. Outcome:

Nowin Utd 2 – Goalless City 1.

Nowin Utd won in injury time

7. Post-match comments:

A well matched game with both teams demonstrating skill on the pitch. Although Goalless managed to keep possession well, Nowin had more shots at goal. The match ended with the tension and excitement of extra time and everything still to play for. Harold Highopes will be very proud of his new team.
Nowin Utd will now be promoted to Division 2 while Goalless City remains in Division 3.

Writing across the Curriculum

A comic strip of the game

1. Introduction	2.	3.
4.	5.	6. Outcome

Use pictures and some written captions to show the main bits of the game.
1 – who/where/when.   2, 3, 4 and 5 – show 4 of the main events (goals or tackles) in the game.
6 – show the outcome of the game (who won/what the score was).

Recording Notes During a Game

1. Teams:

2. Venue:

3. Time/Date:

4. Any comments:

5. Record of events:

a) <u>What happened</u>	b) <u>When</u>	c) <u>Who was involved</u>

6. Outcome:

7. Any comments:

1. – Who is playing? 2. – Where is the game happening? 3. – When is the game happening? 4. – Before the game can you tell who looks like the better team/who is expected to win? Are there any especially talented players on the team? 5. – Record main events as they happen and get all the details (use the back of the sheet if you need more room). 6. – Final score/winners. 7. – After the game were there any surprises? Did the winners deserve it or were they lucky? Which team played better/more fairly?

Sheet H

Writing a recount of a game

Use this framework to help you structure your writing. Remember to look at the checklist to make sure that you are using all the features.

<u>**Opening**</u>
(who, what, where, when)

<u>**Events**</u>
(Write about the main events in the order that they happened.)

<u>**Closing statement**</u>
(Summarise what happened and give the outcome. You can also make some comments about the outcome.)

Unit 2

Lesson focus

History Unit 19 – What were the effects of Tudor exploration?

Overall aim

To write a diary recount of a Tudor exploration from a Tudor's point of view.

History emphasis

In this unit the children learn about the reasons for, and results of, exploration of the world. They are expected to collect information and draw conclusions about life at sea and be able to appreciate the dangers and discomforts of voyages of exploration. They are expected to study one explorer and his explorations in depth.

Literacy links

Year 5, Term 1: T21, T24

About this unit

This unit is probably best done over the course of a week in literacy lessons; any additional time could be 'borrowed' from history/topic lessons. Before starting, the children need to have a sound knowledge of the reasons for, and implications of, Tudor exploration. They should understand that the Tudors were looking for new countries in which to trade wool and other goods, as well as being able to sell expensive, luxury items (such as spices) at home. They should also understand that the Tudors wanted to find places in which to settle. This particular unit of work focuses mainly on how the Tudors explored and they should have read information about life at sea (including navigation, food, superstitions and sea monsters, punishments, daily life and hygiene and disease).

Switching on

Learning objective

- To be able to recognise and identify the features of diary writing.

Resources

- Sheets A and B (pages 22 and 23)
- Selection of diary extracts (these do not need to be linked to the topic but some useful ones include *Pirate Diaries* by Richard Platt and *The diary of a young Tudor lady-in-waiting* by Natalie Grice)

What to do

Briefly revise what the children have done in history on Tudor exploration. Tell them that they are going to look at some diary entries and then eventually write their own diaries in role as a Tudor explorer.

Show them a selection of diaries (see above, plus the usual ones, such as *The Diary of Anne Frank*. You may also want to include a pretend one of your own). Look at a short extract from two or three of these – ask the children to identify things that they think are similar in each one. You may need to prompt them to think about specific areas such as tense, pronouns and connectives.

Share an enlarged version of Sheet B. Read it through together. Ask the children to work in pairs to reread the text and identify **who** it was written by, **where** it was written, **when** it was written, **what** has happened and **why** it has been written. They should also be able to highlight the features from the checklist produced earlier.

Discuss the children's observations, using Sheet A as your guide.

Ask the children to imagine what it might be like to be on the ship – this will help them to prepare for the drama later on in this unit. Ask them how they feel when they go into a very dark place. Discuss why people are afraid of the dark. Raise the issue of how our imaginations conjure up the worst images when faced with the unknown. This was just what it was like for the sailors; no one knew how long the journey would be or whether there would be enough food or even if they would ever return home.

Plenary

With the children's help, create a checklist of features of diary writing to keep for future reference.

Revving up

Learning objectives

■ To develop an understanding of the dangers and discomforts of Tudor exploration.

■ To act in role as a Tudor character.

■ To develop an understanding of diary writing.

Resources

■ Sheets C and D (pages 24 and 25)

■ Checklist of features created in the 'Switching on' lesson

What to do

Explain that each child is going to become a Tudor person on a voyage of exploration! Tell them that they will be working together to produce dramatisations of events that will then be used to help them write their own diary entries in role. If you choose, you may also tell them that the work they produce will be used for display purposes; this may be an added incentive for some.

Introduce and allocate the characters by sharing an enlarged version of Sheet C. There are seven main characters to allow for approximately five working groups in drama. Try to ensure that there is a mixture of abilities within each drama group and also within each character (there will be five of each character) as this will allow the children to inspire and support each other. You will also need to choose a part for yourself in preparation for modelled writing (the character of ship's boy has been used for the exemplar modelled writing).

Cut copies of Sheet D in half and provide the children with a copy of Scenario 1. Read it through together and discuss any questions they may have. Put the children into groups of the same character and give them approximately five minutes to discuss their character's response/actions. Next put them into their drama groups and give them 10 to 15 minutes to plan and dramatise events. You will be able to work with one or two groups and 'shadow' your chosen character.

Bring the class back together. Explain that in the next session they will use their ideas and drama to help them write a diary entry in role. Tell them that today you are going to show them how to write a diary entry and that you will be telling them about what you are thinking as you write so that they can see how writers think – it isn't a big secret and they will find it helpful.

Use the following (if you want) to help you talk to the children as you write, drawing out the features as you write, emphasising personal pronouns and emotions.

The following is a suggestion for a text to use when modelling writing. The children should not see the text but think that you are really making it up as you go along. The idea is that you show them how to write while explaining your thinking at the same time.

The bold print is what you actually write and the italics can be used as a script of what to say to the children.

Okay, I'm a ship's boy. I need to write in the first person as if I was there – I think I'll pretend that I am the same boy who wrote the last diary entry, so it will be the next day... **22nd October 1579**

I'm writing at the end of the day so I need to use the past tense, unless I am thinking about the present or the future as I am writing. **We** *(shows I already feel like part of the crew)* **can no longer see England** *(present tense thoughts)*; **she has been left far behind** *(back in the past tense, retelling events).* **We've worked hard all day. I didn't realise that I could feel so tired.** *Need to mention jobs...* **Everyone has their jobs to do but the ship's boys, like me, seem to get all the dirty jobs. I've scrubbed the decks three times today. I need to keep them clean and stop them getting too slippery and wet – if someone slipped then I would be sure to get a good whipping** *(using what I know from research).* **We didn't get to talk or rest until meal time, and now I wish we hadn't talked so much.** *Present tense 'wish' to show thoughts. I want to* *go on to the stories and show that the crew are superstitious and getting nervous. New paragraph.*

There is a nervousness among the crew; the helmsman thinks the weather will take a turn for the worse and all we can do is wait. *Present tense thinking again; now back to the meal…* **Someone said it was the devil and as we ate there was talk of all the different stories people had heard and believed to be true; tales of terrible sea monsters and vicious natives on strange islands and even a section of the sea that boils and is meant to be so hot that no one can survive the heat.** *Need some more feelings…* **The talk did nothing to settle my uneasiness and although I no longer feel seasick I still wonder if I did the right thing. Life at home was difficult sometimes, what with us being so poor, but at least it was safe.** *Ended on feelings and a bit of a cliffhanger. I am obviously feeling unsafe on the ship.*

Reread through the diary entry. Which bits do the children like? Which bits can be improved? Do they think you have used the features of a diary and included the character's thoughts and feelings?

Plenary

Ask the children to tell you what makes a diary entry different to other kinds of writing, such as a story, for example. Do any of them or their family members write a personal diary? How useful might it be? How helpful is it to read the diaries of people who lived long ago?

Taking off

Learning objectives

■ To be able to empathise with Tudor seafarers.
■ To begin writing own diary entry in role.

Resources

■ Sheet D (page 25)
■ Checklist of diary features

What to do

Remind the children of the work done in the previous lesson. What do they remember about diary writing? Refer to the checklist to reinforce the features.

Provide them with a copy of Scenario 2 from Sheet D. Read it through together. As in the 'Revving up' session, put them into character groups and let them discuss what their character might do/say/feel. After a suitable time (approximately five minutes) organise them into their drama groups/crews.

Allow 10 to 15 minutes for the children to work together to dramatise events from the scenario. Spend a little time working with the groups, supporting actions and giving ideas and advice as necessary.

Bring the class back together and explain that they are now going to write their own personal diary entry as their character. Remind them that they need to include some facts about events as well as lots of their own personal feelings. Tell them that they can be imaginative and that their diary should be written as if they are actually speaking to it (more like thinking out loud really). Display the checklist of features and remind the children to refer to this as they write.

Give the children 20 to 30 minutes to write their diary entries. Depending on the class, you may want to let them share ideas and help each other or you may wish them to work totally individually. You will be able to work with your weaker writers to help scaffold their compositions, reminding them of the expectations and required features. It may be possible to spend your time with a particular character and write a group entry, using their ideas as you scribe.

After 20 to 30 minutes ask the children to swap their work with each other. They can then spend ten minutes or so 'marking' each other's work. When encouraging them to peer mark it is important to give them a framework (such as the checklist) and ensure that they are positive and not overly critical. The success of this exercise will depend on the class and their experience. Once practised, peer marking is an invaluable skill that has great benefits for both marker and 'markee'.

Plenary

Discuss how helpful the drama session was in helping them to write in role. Did it help them to understand the character better? What problems did they have when trying to write in role? How did they overcome these problems?

Flying solo

Learning objective

■ To be able to communicate their knowledge and understanding of Tudor exploration and life at sea in the form of a Tudor diary.

Resources

■ Examples of children's diary writing on OHTs
■ Checklist of features
■ Previous work
■ Selection of information books about Tudor voyages of exploration

What to do

Show two or three good examples of the children's writing from the 'Taking off' session. Look at them with the class. Ask each child to choose one thing that the writer has done really well. The children can record their responses on dry wipe boards and then show you their answers. Pick out some of their observations and ask them to justify their thoughts, using evidence from the writing. Now do the same again but ask the children for one thing that they think the writer could improve on. Again, get them to show you their answers. When everyone has made an observation ask them to think about how they would improve the thing they have chosen. Discuss ideas and take responses orally.

Get the children into their drama groups/crews. Tell them that today they will be creating their own scenario to write their diary about. Use the information books to give them some ideas and suggestions before letting them get started. Allow 20 minutes or so to plan and practise their dramatisations.

Ask each group to select a spokesperson to give a brief summary of events to the audience to set the scene. (This can be presented in a similar format to the scenarios provided.)

Each group should then present their scenario in turn.

Following on from the performances, the children can write their diary entry in the same way as yesterday.

Diary entries can be edited and proofread for homework and could be presented for display. It might be fun to have a go at making the paper look old (tea bags and singed corners ahoy!) in order to make an impressive display complete with facts and other information and maps of Tudor exploration.

If possible the children should be given the opportunity to share their work, perhaps by choosing their better diary entry and sharing it with the class.

Plenary

Tell the children you would like them to develop a 'hints' sheet for other Year 5 children on how to write a diary entry. Ask them for suggestions for the best hints they can think of. The hints can include things from the checklist as well as ideas for making the writing interesting, such as including information about the person's feelings and emotions/reactions to situations. If appropriate, make the sheet available to the other Year 5 class to use.

date

We don't know who the boy is but we are given some information about him.

21st October, 1579

first person

Well, I finally went and did it! Only this morning I left the farm and my family and now I find myself on board a real ship! With me gone, Ma and Pa won't have so many mouths to feed. They've looked after me for ten years. Now it's time to look after myself.

It was amazing seeing the sea for the first time. I've heard stories but I didn't know how beautiful it was. I could barely contain my excitement. As I was hungry I stopped at an inn for some pease pudding and ale. The landlord was a jolly chap and when I told him of my wish to go to sea he took me out in his boat and rowed me out to a ship in the harbour where he knew one of the men on board.

interesting details

past tense

The wooden ship was breathtaking. Everything was strange and new and everywhere people were busy. There were quite a few boys about my age and one of them, Weasel, took me to the slop chest to get the right clothes for the voyage. My breeches were alright but I had to give up my boots and go barefoot. Inside the crew's quarters it was dark and the heat was stifling. Our first meal was of bread and cheese, with dried fish and salted meat, all washed down with ale.

events in chronological order

time connective

After our meal the bos'n's whistle called all the men to their stations. I went to help Weasel get the anchor up. It was slow, heavy work and when the anchor came up it was covered with weed and stank of slime. While the sails were being set I was given a brush and bucket to clean the mess off the deck where the muddy water had dripped.

Now I am exhausted and as the ship rolls I have an odd feeling in my stomach. I wonder if I have done the right thing.

present tense used to show thoughts as he is writing

21st October, 1579

Well, I finally went and did it!
Only this morning I left the farm
and my family and now I find
myself on board a real ship! With
me gone, Ma and Pa won't have so
many mouths to feed. They've
looked after me for ten years. Now
it's time to look after myself.

It was amazing seeing the sea for
the first time. I've heard stories but
I didn't know how beautiful it was.
I could barely contain my excitement. As I was hungry I stopped at an
inn for some pease pudding and ale. The landlord was a jolly chap
and when I told him of my wish to go to sea he took me out in his boat
and rowed me out to a ship in the harbour where he knew one of the
men on board.

The wooden ship was breathtaking. Everything was strange and new
and everywhere people were busy. There were quite a few boys about my
age and one of them, Weasel, took me to the slop chest to get the right
clothes for the voyage. My breeches were alright but I had to give up my
boots and go barefoot. Inside the crew's quarters it was dark and the
heat was stifling. Our first meal was of bread and cheese, with dried
fish and salted meat, all washed down with ale.

After our meal the bos'n's whistle called all the men to their stations. I
went to help Weasel get the anchor up. It was slow, heavy work and
when the anchor came up it was covered with weed and stank of slime.
While the sails were being set I was given a brush and bucket to clean
the mess off the deck where the muddy water had dripped.

Now I am exhausted and as the ship rolls I have an odd feeling in my
stomach. I wonder if I have done the right thing.

List of characters

Captain – in charge of the ship and the crew, responsible for the voyage.

First Mate – takes orders from the captain and manages the ship. Commands the ship when the captain is sleeping.

Helmsman – sailor who steers the ship; follows instructions from the captain and first mate.

Lookout – sailor who sits in the crow's-nest and keeps an eye out for land, ice and other ships.

Ship's boy – young boy who does general jobs. Helps when he is needed and does as he is told. May spend time as a cabin boy if he can read and write.

Cabin boy – works closely with the captain and first mate. He may be required to write in the ship's log. He also runs more specific errands.

Powder monkey – one of the ship's boys who is responsible for carrying the gunpowder to the cannons as well as keeping the stores safe and dry.

NB: the captain and first mate will have their own private cabins to sleep and eat meals in. The rest of the crew share the crew's quarters below deck.

Scenario 1

It is the start of the voyage. The ship has set sail and the coast of England is no longer visible – all around is grey sea and sky. You begin to worry that a storm is on the way. All the crew are busy; the captain and first mate stand with the helmsman, navigating the ship and plotting their course, the lookout is high above in the crow's-nest and the crew are cleaning, preparing and generally hard at work.

The weather takes a turn for the worse. Nerves run high as you remember the stories of sea monsters, ferocious tribes and freezing or boiling seas. As you realise that you really are sailing into the unknown you begin to wonder if this was such a good idea.

Scenario 2

You've been at sea for a few months now. You have seen several strange and wonderful creatures. The conditions on ship are cramped and the crew have taken to sleeping on deck when the weather is fine. You're working hard and you end each day exhausted.

The food rations are very low, the bread has run out and you have to eat dry biscuits. The dried fish and salted meat taste horrid and do not provide a balanced diet. Lots of the sailors are suffering from scurvy due to lack of vitamin C and one or two have died. There is still a small amount of ale left but everything else is mouldy – even the water has turned green. The sailors are starting to become jealous of the captain, who always gets the best food and ale. Carrying out your daily chores becomes increasingly difficult as your body becomes hungrier and weaker. No one knows how much longer you will be at sea and when you finally do reach land, no one knows what you will find when you go ashore.

Chapter 2

Report writing

What is a report text?

A report is a non-chronological text written to describe or classify something. It brings together a set of related information and sorts it into paragraphs of closely connected facts. Reports can also be used to compare and contrast.

Structural features

- Usually begins with an introduction to orientate the reader. Tells us 'who', 'what', 'where' and 'when'
- Main body of text is organised into paragraphs describing particular aspects of the subject
- Ends with a conclusion that briefly summarises the text
- Non-chronological

Linguistic features

- Often written in the present tense (except for historical reports)
- Usually uses generic nouns and pronouns (such as people, cats, buildings) rather than specific ones
- Written in an impersonal third person style
- Factual writing often using technical words
- Language is used to describe and differentiate
- Linking words and phrases are used
- Occasional use of the passive

Examples of reports

- non-fiction books
- newspaper/magazine articles
- information leaflets, tourist guidebooks

Teaching report writing

Writing a non-chronological report is a bit like collecting shells on the beach in a bucket and then sorting them into piles of similar shells, discarding anything that is damaged or has been scooped up that isn't a shell!

Children need to learn to gather from research relevant information about the subject they are going to describe, sort the information into groups of facts that go together and then link them in a logical order, both within the paragraphs and between the paragraphs. They have to learn how to 'file' information into these paragraphs so that the reader can access the information easily and logically. Using subheadings for paragraphs can help children organise their information. They need to choose which information is most important to the reader and elaborate on it.

One of the difficulties for children is to be able to research the information they need without simply copying out (or printing out) passages from reference sources. They need to be taught how to select key words and phrases and use them in their own sentences.

Report writing – progression

Simple non-chronological reports are introduced in Key Stage 1 (Year 1, Term 2: T25; Year 2, Term 3: T21).

In Year 3 children locate information in non-fiction books using the text structures – contents, index, headings, subheadings, page numbers and bibliographies. They record information from texts and write simple non-chronological reports for a known audience (Term 1: T17, T18, T21, T22).

In Year 4 children identify different types of text and different features of non-fiction texts in print and IT (Term 1: T16, T17) and they write non-chronological reports, including the use of organisational devices (Term 1: T21).

In **Year 5** (Term 1: T26; Term 2: T22) children learn to make notes for different purposes and to plan, compose, edit and refine short non-chronological texts.

In Year 6 (Term 1: T17; Term 3: T19, T22) children are moving on to writing non-chronological reports linked to other subjects. They review a range of text features and select the appropriate style and form to suit a specific purpose and audience.

Unit 1

Lesson focus

Religious Education Unit 5B – How do Muslims express their beliefs through practices?

Overall aim

To write a non-chronological report about some of the Five Pillars of Islam.

Religious Education emphasis

Children are learning about the most important beliefs in Islam and how these are expressed through practices such as prayer and fasting. They are identifying, understanding and considering the significance to believers of the teachings found in the Qur'an. They will develop their existing skills of research, notetaking and organising information into cohesive descriptive paragraphs to write a non-chronological report about some of the Five Pillars of Islam: *Shahadah* (statement of belief), Salah (prayer), *Sawm* (fasting), *Zakaah* (giving alms) and *Hajj* (pilgrimage). While appreciating the beliefs of Muslims the children may also reflect on beliefs they themselves hold to be important and how these affect their own actions.

Literacy links

Year 5, Term 2: T16, T17, T19, T20 T21, T22, T23

About this unit

The following lessons will probably work best if you have previously given the children some introduction to the Islamic faith.

This unit can be done as a creative project linking RE and literacy. In this way the distinctions between literacy and RE would be blurred to create a more holistic learning experience. Alternatively, the research could be done in RE and drawn upon in a literacy session, when the non-chronological report can be written. The children will need access to a variety of sources of information about the Five Pillars of Islam, including IT sources such as CD-Roms, videos and relevant internet links. Writing non-chronological reports at this level is demanding and the children will benefit from a strong underpinning of talking about their note taking and writing with response partners before, during and after writing.

Switching on

Learning objectives

- To identify the linguistic and structural features of a non-chronological report.
- To know the Qur'an is a holy book and that the Five Pillars of Islam are found within it.
- To revisit the ways Muslims express through practices their beliefs, ideas and feelings.

Resources

- Sheets A and B (pages 33 and 34)
- Some relevant religious artefacts, such as a Qur'an and a stand
- A photograph album of your own

What to do

Tell the children you have brought something very special with you to school. Tell them it is a book that you and your family treasure at home. Very carefully produce a photograph album. Tell them it is a very special book to you and it has special pictures of things and events that are important to your life, such as when you were a baby, your wedding, when you passed your driving test and your grandparents. Tell them that many of these pictures tell a story that is important to you. Ask them if they have any special books and to say why the books are important to them. Explain that people of different faiths have special books that are very important to them.

Show the children the Qur'an and explain that it is a special book that Muslims treat with great respect. Tell them it is a book that teaches Muslims how to live their lives. It helps them to know how to worship, how they should treat others and how they should treat their environment. Place the Qur'an on a stand and let the children see it.

Tell the children that the Qur'an has some beliefs and rules that Muslims believe are very important and they try to live by them. They are called the Five Pillars of Islam. They are called pillars because they are so important that a Muslim's life rests upon them and is supported by them in the way a magnificent building is supported by pillars. You might show a picture of a building with prominent pillars to illustrate the point.

Either introduce or, better, refresh their memory about Shahadah (profession of faith). Tell them it is a very important statement of belief for Muslims. It is the most important pillar of faith and it has two parts so that a Muslim can profess they believe in only one god and Muhammad (peace be upon him) is a prophet of God.

Explain that the most important pillar after Shahadah is Salah (prayer). Prayer is the way Muslims communicate with God. They pray five times a day if they can and there are special things they must do when they pray, such as washing and adopting particular postures. They do this because they believe God has given them everything and they must be thankful and remember and worship him. Muslims believe prayer helps them to be aware of God all the time and helps them to be good people.

Give them a chance to talk about all these things and to ask questions. Now ask the children to think of anything they believe in really strongly. Tell them that what we believe can lead to our taking certain actions.

Say that another of the rules is about giving money to needy people. Muslims call this rule Zakaah.

Now show the children an enlarged version of Sheet B (page 34). Tell them they are going to read a non-chronological report about the Five Pillars of Islam which includes information about Zakaah and Shahadah. Say that they will use this as a model for their own writing later.

Read the text with the children and discuss any questions or consider any thoughts they might have about the Five Pillars of Islam, especially Zakaah and Shahadah. Questions might include:

- Do they know anyone who gives money to needy people?
- What beliefs make them choose to give their money away?
- What good does it do?
- How do people who receive the money feel?
- Why do Muslims say Shahadah words first thing in the morning and last thing at night?
- Do you say any special words in your house?

Now carefully point out how the report has been constructed. You can use the annotations on Sheet A to help you.

Ask the children to work with a partner and to think of three important points to remember about writing a non-chronological report. They can write them down on a dry wipe board. Ask them to tell you their responses and make a bullet pointed list of them for when they write their own non-chronological report. Display this prominently in the classroom so they can use it as a reminder.

Plenary

Do some simple drama around the practice of Zakaah. Tell the children to make small groups and create a small tableau or freeze-frame of a person in need receiving money as a result of Zakaah. Let all the children see each other's tableau. Ask them what they have learned about Zakaah.

Revving up

Learning objectives

- ■ To know that going on a long journey (a pilgrimage) is one of many ways that religious beliefs can be expressed.
- ■ To make notes.

Resources

- ■ Sheets C, D, E and F (pages 35 to 38)
- ■ A range of suitable sources, both printed and electronic, about Sawm and Salah
- ■ Video, photographs, visiting speakers, artefacts about the Five Pillars

What to do

Tell the children that they are now going to gather together all the information they will need to write their own non-chronological report about the Five Pillars of Islam. Tell them that first they are going to find out about Hajj. They will have to read some sources and make notes. Ask them to discuss in pairs what they already know about Hajj.

Share enlarged versions of Sheets C, D and E. Discuss the children's understanding of what happens at Hajj. Ask questions such as:

- • Why do Muslims go to Makkah?
- • Why do they throw stones at the three pillars?
- • What do people wear for the Hajj?
- • Why is it so special for Muslims?
- • What difference do you think it will make when they return home?

Show the children how to highlight key words or phrases in the text in order to make a summary of the information. For example, in the text of the telephone call they should ignore the first two sentences but highlight 'wear only two white sheets of seamless cloth'.

Give the children their own copies of Sheets C, D and E. Ask them to work in pairs to underline or highlight important pieces of information about Hajj. They may need 20 minutes for this. When they are ready ask them to share their information with another pair, referring to their highlighted words.

Ask each pair to write down one fact about Hajj on a large strip of paper. Bring the class back together and pin all the strips of paper to the board. Together, sort these strips under the following headings:

- • Why people go on a Hajj
- • What people wear on a Hajj
- • What people do on a Hajj

Read through the facts pinned to the board. Ask the children to tell you if there are any important facts that are missing.

Now ask the children to write the facts on their note taking grid (Sheet F).

Before carrying out the next lesson ('Taking off'), provide the children with reference sources about the other four pillars and ask them to make notes in the same way for each one and add their notes to the grid.

They could watch a video about the Five Pillars or a parent or local Muslim representative might be invited into school to talk about them.

Plenary

Discuss with the children some of the challenges they faced when making notes and ask them if they thought some sources were better than others and if this has any implications for research, such as the importance of reading more than one text and evaluating their usefulness.

Catherine packed her bag <u>carefully</u>.	opposite the bus stop
She will arrive <u>soon</u>.	with great care
I will meet you <u>at that place.</u>	in a few days' time

Taking off

Learning objectives

■ To know how to write a non-chronological report.
■ To understand adverbial phrases.

Resources

■ A child's completed note taking grid (Sheet F)
■ Hand held dry wipe boards

What to do

Spend a few minutes reminding the children what an adverbial phrase is. Agree that it is a group of words that does the same job as a single adverb; adverbial phrases give extra meaning to verbs. They can give information about when, where and how something happens.

Show them the sentence:

Mum will be leaving in a few days' time.

Highlight 'in a few days' time'. Tell them this is an adverbial phrase because, just like an adverb, it tells you when Mum will be leaving. Now show them the next sentence.

Philip ran as fast as possible.

Highlight 'as fast as possible'. Tell them this is an adverbial phrase because, just like an adverb, it tells you how Philip ran.

Write the following sentences on the board and ask the children to match the adverbs underlined with the three adverbial phrases.

Tell them they have one minute to work with a partner to make up as many sentences with adverbial phrases as they can. After one minute ask them to tell their best sentence with an adverbial phrase to another pair. The listeners must identify the adverbial phrase. Take some feedback.

Tell the children that they are going to write their own non-chronological reports about the Five Pillars of Islam, but before they begin you are going to do some writing on the board using the notes they made in the last session. This is so they can learn from you how such writing is done.

Enlarge one child's completed Sheet F and refer to it as you write.

Tell them they will need to refer to the bullet pointed list from the 'Switching on' session of all the things they need to remember when they write their own non-chronological report and that you will be referring to it as you write.

Consider with the children who the audience might be (such as another class). Then begin to demonstrate to the children how you could write a non-chronological report.

Write on the flip chart, whiteboard or OHT in front of them, speaking as you write. It is best to write only a few sentences on your own and then involve the children's ideas. You will need to work from the children's notes to demonstrate the importance of referring to their notes but the script below might help you to get started. The script is for your eyes only. What you say is in italics; what you write is in bold.

I am going to write the beginning of a non-chronological report about the Five Pillars of Islam. I am only going to write mostly about Hajj, Sawm and Salah. Watch what I am doing and listen to how I am thinking through the writing.

Let me put the title so the reader knows what the report is about – **The Five Pillars of Islam**. *Now I need an introductory sentence or two that tell the reader generally* *what the the Five Pillars of Islam are before I get into the detail of Hajj, Salah and Sawm. What about simply –* **There are five pillars of faith that Muslims try to live by.***?*

Now I need to give a bit more information to say what they are, tell the reader that they are rules. I think just saying 'They are practices,' is a bit weak and not helpful. Let me think. Hmm. What about – **They are practices that help them to live out the things that they believe.***? Now I can introduce the three I am going to focus on.* **The Pillars of Islam are Shahadah, Salah Zakaah, Hajj and Sawm.** *Let's read it back. Hmm. It sounds good.*

I will start a new paragraph. I want to tell the reader clearly that Shahadah is the most important and is a belief. This is quite a hard sentence to construct so I need to think a little. What about – **Shahada is the most important pillar. It means Muslims must state they believe in only one god and that Muhammad (peace be upon him) is a prophet of God.***? Let's read it back. I am writing 'peace be upon him' after the word Muhammad because that is what Muslims do and it shows my respect for their beliefs. Now I just need to say* **The other pillars are ways of living out these beliefs.**

I can put a subheading here if I want. I think I shall. **<u>Hajj</u>** *Now I want to tell the reader what a Hajj is.* **Hajj is a pilgrimage.** *Let's read it back. I think it is too short. The reader needs a bit more information. What about* **All Muslims try to go on a pilgrimage to Makkah…** *let's put an adverbial phrase here …***at least once in their life. This is called Hajj.** *That's great. Will the reader know what a pilgrimage is? Perhaps I'd better add* **This pilgrimage is a special journey religious people make.**

Now I need to say why they go. What about – **Muslims go because it is one of the pillars of faith and it strengthens their belief. They feel closer to God and to other Muslims.***? Let's read it back from the beginning. Hmm. I think it will work.*

Now that you have shown the children how to begin, ask them to help compose the next paragraph. They could give you ideas or write it themselves in pairs or on hand held whiteboards.

Plenary

Show the children how you can move around in the sentence adverbial phrases that tell you 'when'. Say to the children when reading the sentence back *'Look, if I want I can put "at least once in their life" at the front of this sentence for variety.'* Tell the more able children that you expect them to try this in their own writing.

Flying solo

Learning objectives

■ To write a non-chronological report using notes.

■ To revise understanding of sorting information into paragraphs.

■ To revise understanding of adverbial phrases.

Resource

■ Completed note taking grids (Sheet F)

What to do

Make sure the children have copies of their note taking grids (Sheet F) and tell them that they are going to write their own non-chronological report independently, emphasising that they must refer to their notes. Remind them to refer to the lists of key structural and linguistic features you have displayed on the wall. Set small targets for some groups. Remind them of any personal literacy targets.

Remind them that one sequence for writing is:

• Gather your ideas;
• Rehearse your sentence;
• Write sentence down;
• Read back and make any changes.

Remind the children that they need to gather sentences together under subheadings so that they are organised into paragraphs, just as they did in the last session.

Tell more able children that you expect them to attempt to put an adverbial phrase at the beginning of a sentence for variety.

Provide a list of key words for the less able. They can refer to this as they write their report. You may want to make a little key of symbols next to each key word, such as a dome shape next to the word 'mosque'.

Stop the children at intervals during their independent writing to share their non-chronological report with a response partner. As they read their writing aloud they will notice gaps and where the writing doesn't flow and self-correct. Ask the children to give at least two positive comments about their partner's writing and one idea for refining it.

Differentiate your expectations and make them clear to the children. They might follow the outline below:

Must = write a report on one pillar, for example on fasting.

Should = write a report using their notes on fasting, prayer and pilgrimage.

Could = write a report on all five pillars using adverbial phrases, their own notes from a variety of texts and a correct report structure

Guided writing
Work intensively with the more able group. Read through two or three of their reports so far. Work all together on one report at a time. Try to let the children do most of the talking.

- Give each child a copy of the report to be discussed if you can (you may need to quickly photocopy it).
- Ask the author to read out his or her paragraph(s).
- Ask the children to underline in one colour three things that work well for the reader; for example, a good title and strong vocabulary.
- Let the children explain to the author these positive points. Encourage the author to say why he or she made those choices and elaborate as much as they can.
- Introduce your own supportive comments appropriately – remember, feedback from a peer is very powerful.

- Now ask the children to underline one or two things the author could change to make it better for the reader (they can work in pairs – you want to encourage as much talk as possible).
- Invite the children to make their suggestions, ensuring it is in an appropriate and positive way, and discuss the effects their suggested changes will have. Extend the children's ideas and invite the author to respond. Offer the author time to make changes on his or her draft there and then, while you begin work on another author's report. It does not matter if you do not get through all the children. You can reach them in the next guided reading session. Make some notes so you can return to those you missed during the next session.

Plenary

Earlier in the day, tell two or three children that you are going to ask them to read out their reports. (They could have written them directly onto an OHT.) Give them some time to practise. Bring the children together at plenary time. After the children have read their reports, ask them to say what they are pleased with. Then discuss with all the children what was challenging and what they have learned about writing a non-chronological report. Praise the children.

title
to indicate what the report is about

introduction tells the reader what the report is going to be about

The Five Pillars of Islam

adverbial phrase for 'how'

The Qur'an is a holy book for Muslims and it is treated with the greatest respect. Muslims believe it is the word of God and it tells them what they can do to live a good life. Within the Qur'an there are some practices called the Five Pillars of Faith, which Muslims try to follow. These pillars are called Shahadah (statement of belief), Salah (prayer), Zakaah (giving alms), Sawm (fasting) and Hajj (pilgrimage).

third person

The first pillar is Shahadah and it is the most important one. It means the profession of faith. Muslims think that it is important to declare what they believe and they say the words 'La ilaha illal Lah, Muhammad Rasulullah' which means in English 'There is no other god but Allah and Muhammad is the prophet of Allah.' These words are very special to Muslims and they can be the first words they say when they wake up and the last words when they go to bed. These will be the first words a newborn baby hears because the parents will whisper them into the baby's ear.

organised in paragraphs

present tense

The next most important pillar is Salah, which means prayer. Muslims believe prayer keeps them aware of God all the time and pray five times a day.

adverbial phrase for 'where'.

Giving money to people who are in need is another pillar of faith and this act is called Zakaah. Muslims believe everything they have, including money, belongs to God, and it should be used in ways God would approve of. The money might go to people who are sick or poor, or people who are without a home. Money can also be given to charitable organisations. Sometimes it will be given openly as a form of encouragement to others but mostly it is given privately. Muslims also give money over and above Zakaah out of goodwill to charities.

adverbial phrase for 'when'

facts, not opinions

Another pillar of faith is Sawm which means fasting. For short periods, Muslims will not have food or drink from dawn until sundown. Muslims believe this helps them to become more aware of the presence of God.

Hajj is a pillar of faith. Hajj is a journey where Muslims from all parts of the world come together in Makkah to renew their faith in God. Muslims will try to perform Hajj once in their lifetime if they have money and good health.

Shahadah, then, is a statement of belief and it is the most important pillar of faith while the other pillars – Salah, Sawm, Zakaah and Hajj – are ways that a Muslim's beliefs lead to actions.

conclusion rounds off the report

The Five Pillars of Islam

The Qur'an is a holy book for Muslims and it is treated with the greatest respect. Muslims believe it is the word of God and it tells them what they can do to live a good life. Within the Qur'an there are some practices called the Five Pillars of Faith, which Muslims try to follow. These pillars are called Shahadah (statement of belief), Salah (prayer), Zakaah (giving alms), Sawm (fasting) and Hajj (pilgrimage).

The first pillar is Shahadah and it is the most important one. It means the profession of faith. Muslims think that it is important to declare what they believe and they say the words 'La ilaha illal Lah, Muhammad Rasulullah' which means in English 'There is no other god but Allah and Muhammad is the prophet of Allah.' These words are very special to Muslims and they can be the first words they say when they wake up and the last words when they go to bed. These will be the first words a newborn baby hears because the parents will whisper them into the baby's ear.

The next most important pillar is Salah, which means prayer. Muslims believe prayer keeps them aware of God all the time and pray five times a day.

Giving money to people who are in need is another pillar of faith and this act is called Zakaah. Muslims believe everything they have, including money, belongs to God, and it should be used in ways God would approve of. The money might go to people who are sick or poor, or people who are without a home. Money can also be given to charitable organisations. Sometimes it will be given openly as a form of encouragement to others but mostly it is given privately. Muslims also give money over and above Zakaah out of goodwill to charities.

Another pillar of faith is Sawm, which means fasting. For short periods, Muslims will not have food and drink from dawn until sundown. Muslims believe this helps them to become more aware of the presence of God.

Hajj is a pillar of faith. Hajj is a journey where Muslims from all parts of the world come together in Makkah to renew their faith in God. Muslims will try to perform Hajj once in their lifetime if they have money and good health.

Shahadah, then, is a statement of belief and it is the most important pillar of faith, while the other pillars – Salah, Sawm, Zakaah and Hajj – are ways that a Muslim's beliefs lead to actions.

The Hajj

Telephone call to a child from a relative

'I am so pleased you are able to go on the Hajj. Now remember what I told you. You must wear only two white sheets of seamless cloth so no one can tell if you are rich or poor, young or old, like the other men. You only need to do this for the three days you do the rituals. Everyone must look alike. The women, of course, can wear normal clothes as long as they are covered from head to ankles and they must keep their face uncovered so their face shows. Everyone is equal on the Hajj. Okay. Also, if you take your soaps and perfumes remember you can't use them for the three days of the ritual. Oh… and don't cut your hair or nails during these days either. I only want you to get the most from it. I know you have saved up for it. Every Muslim should go on the Hajj once if they can afford it. You know I should not go because my family would suffer if I went. Have a lovely time and tell me everything that happens. Hajj will please God and deepen your faith.'

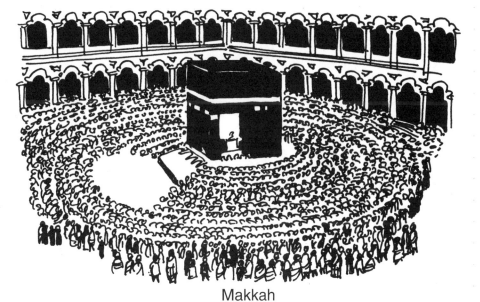

Makkah

Diary of a child on Hajj

There are so many people here. I understand what Mufti meant when he said there are two million people who come here each year. So much has happened. I walked seven times around the Ka'bah and I walked seven times between the hills of Safa and Marwa. This reminded us all of the story of Hagar who was the mother of Ishmael (Peace be upon him). She ran up and down the hills looking desperately for water for them both until God made water flow from the holy well of Zamzam. I was tired in the heat though. Sometimes it reached nearly 50 degrees.

It was very special for me to throw the pebbles at the three stone pillars. I really wanted to show that I rejected evil and wanted to follow God, just like Ishmael (Peace be upon him) drove the devil away by throwing stones at him, as the Qur'an teaches us.

I didn't see the sacrifice of a sheep in the final festival but I understood why. It is a symbol of being willing to give up our lives and possessions for God while we are on Earth. We ate some of the meat afterwards but a lot of it was given to the poor people. I am glad I came. I really feel a sense of unity with other Muslims all over the world. I feel very moved.

A Hajj pilgrim's schedule

Arrive some days before in Makkah and prepare by praying.

Day 1: After sunrise leave Makkah and go to Mena by walking, bus or car. Stay in this valley between two hills and pray during the day. Relax in preparation for the next part of Hajj and sleep in Mena at night.

Day 2: This is the most important day of Hajj. Go to Arafat by walking, bus or car. Spend day praying, asking God's forgiveness and seeking God's pleasure. Leave after sunset and go to Muzdalifah. Spend night sleeping in open at Muzdalifah. Collect 49 small pebbles.

Day 3: Return to Mena. Stone the one pillar of Satan as a symbol of saying Satan is coming between you and God and you do not want that. Animals sacrificed to remember Abraham (Peace be upon him) and food distributed to the poor. Men cut hair after sacrifice and women cut one inch of hair.

In the evening go back to Makkah and walk around Ka'bah seven times. Drink Zamzam water and pray. Walk between the two hills of Safa and Marwa seven times. Return to Mena the same night.

Day 4: Stay in Mena and rest. After midday stone each of the three pillars with seven stones each to celebrate Abraham's faith (Peace be upon him).

Day 5: Stay in Mena and rest until midday. After midday throw the remaining stones at the pillars and then leave before sunset

After Hajj go to Madinah where Muhammad (Peace be upon him) is buried and give praise, blessings and salutations.

The Five Pillars of Islam

Shahadah	Salah	Zakaah	Sawm	Hajj

Unit 2

Lesson focus

Geography Unit 11 – Water

Overall aim

To write a non-chronological report about a comparison between how water is used in this country and a less economically developed country.

Geography emphasis

The children will learn how water is used in the world. They will investigate similarities and differences between the way they use water and the way people in less economically developed countries use water. They will understand that where people live affects water distribution and access to water. They will develop some geographical enquiry skills, such as using maps and atlases. They will develop some research skills using ICT.

Literacy links

Year 5, Term 2: T20, T22, T24, S3, S9

About this unit

This unit should sit neatly within a range of teaching units about water, such as the comparison of different localities. The work described here might best be done by combining geography and literacy lessons so that the objectives are explicitly met in a more cohesive single project. The children will work towards producing a non-comparative report for a football programme.

Switching on

Learning objectives

- To gather information about use of water in children's own homes and in less economically developed countries.
- To make notes.

Resources

- Sheets A, B and C (pages 45 to 47)
- A recent match programme from the local football team to show the children the type of publication they will be writing for, and suggest purpose and audience for the writing
- Websites, including *www.wateraid.org.uk*
- Tearfund video 'Water Forecast 2000' (Tel: 08453 558355)

Note: this lesson is best spread over at least two sessions to give the children time to do the research at home about their own water use.

What to do

Tell the children that the local football club has been working with the local water authority and is running a 'Save water' campaign throughout the next season. At each home match they will be using the scoreboard and the match programme to give fans tips on how to make the most of their water. The football club has asked your class to write a double page spread for one of their future match programmes. Show them a copy of a programme if you can.

Tell the children that the manager wants them to write about the differences and similarities in the way they use water in their own homes and the way children in less economically developed countries use water in their homes. Help them to use an atlas to find where less economically developed countries are.

Say that they are going to set some questions, research books, leaflets and internet sites and make some notes on grids in order to help them compare the different ways water is used.

Ask them what they already know about the way they use water and the way children in other, less economically developed, countries use water. Together, think of some questions about water use they could research. The following questions could apply to either themselves or children in a less economically developed country:

• Where do I/they get water from in the house?
• How many points of access to water do I/they have?
• What do I/they use clean water for?
• How much water do I/they use?
• Where does the water I/they use come from?
• Why do I/they need clean water?

Set the children a homework task using Sheet A (page 45). Write the questions they have to answer on the dotted lines. (They could be some of the questions the children asked earlier.) Tell them to complete the information in the ovals on children in less economically developed countries if they can, but not to worry if they can't because they will complete those anyway at school. You may want to scan and download this sheet on your school computer system so that you can use it on the interactive whiteboard or as templates on word processors.

After the children have done their homework, organise them into small groups to discuss their findings about their *own* water use at home. Ask each group to select a spokesperson to feed back some of the main points. Spend a few minutes listening to the spokespeople and discuss the findings.

Tell the children they must now use books, leaflets and internet sites to find out how children in less economically developed countries use water. They should make notes as they go. Give the children copies of Sheet B (page 46) to read through.

If possible use visual aids, such as those listed in the Resources section.

If the children are using the internet you may need to discourage them from simply printing everything they see. One way is to open simultaneously both the internet site and a new word processing document. The children, working in pairs, can then highlight the useful sentences from the webpage and paste them into the word processing document. This can then be printed and used as part of the valuable research that can contribute to their writing.

Finally, show the children how to use Sheet C to record the differences they have found.

Plenary

Take some feedback from the children about the facts they have found out. Discuss how they would feel if they had to carry all the water they use to their house rather than just open the tap. Fill some plastic bottles with water and let them feel the weight of one flush of the toilet (15 litres).

Revving up

Learning objectives

■ To know the key features of a comparative report.
■ To know how to use commas when using a relative clause.

Resources

■ The children's notes made in the previous session
■ Some speech bubbles drawn on paper and cut out

What to do

Spend some time showing the children how to use a relative clause. Explain that a relative clause is a piece of information about someone or something that can be dropped into the middle of a sentence. It contains a verb. Tell them that relative clauses often begin with 'who' or 'which'. Show them some sentences such as those below written on a long piece of cardboard:

Mummy uses a lot of water.
The water comes out of taps in our house.

Cut one sentence in half and drop in another card with a relative clause on it. For example:

Mummy, **who washes my clothes,** uses a lot of water.

The water, **which is always clean,** comes out of taps in our house.

Point out that the relative clause needs commas on either side of it. Ask the children to make up some more in pairs and share them.

Now tell the children they are going to find out how to write a comparative report and that they will be writing one about the use of water. They will need all the notes they have made so far. Remind them of any recent reports they have written in other curriculum areas.

Ask the children to discuss in pairs what they already know about writing reports and then feed that back as a whole class. Make a list of these features under the heading 'A really good report'. The list should include:

- begins with a statement to tell the reader what the report is about;
- is written impersonally;
- usually has facts;
- has a variety of sentence openings;
- has information organised into paragraphs about the same subject;
- does not have personal opinions;
- has a conclusion to sum up the text.

Explain that the report they are going to write will be a comparative one. It will have all the features in the list above but will also include sentences that compare one thing with another. Say that they are now going to do an activity with a partner to show them how to do this.

Ask them to discuss with a partner some differences and similarities; for example, their appearance, their houses and their interests.

Then ask the pairs to jot down some notes on a hand held whiteboard in a frame such as the one below:

	Child A	Child B
appearance house interests		

Ask them now to make spoken paragraphs by speaking to each other using the headings and the notes. You may want to model this yourself; for example: *'I live in a flat with a good view of the town but Peter lives in a house with a large garden with a swing in it.'*

Some children may benefit from working with a teaching assistant to tape record their spoken sentences and listen to what they have said.

Ask the children to reflect on what makes a good paragraph that compares things. Ask them to think of a good thing their partner said.

Tell them that good comparative reports have all the information comparing the same things together in the same paragraph and they will use words such as 'however', 'although', 'instead' and 'as well' to link the sentences together. Explain that words such as these are called 'connectives'.

Tell the children that you are going to write on the board a non-chronological report comparing the life of a teacher from Britain with the life of a teacher from a distant country, such as Japan, or even an imaginary country or planet. This could be quite humorous if you invite the children's ideas. Collect their ideas on a simple comparative grid:

	Britain	Planet Tharg
Clothes Classrooms		

As you write the report, talk about what you are writing as if you are thinking to yourself. (The text in italics is what you say; the bold is what you write.) Identify the things you are doing from the list above that makes it a really good comparative report.

Now, I will start the non-chronological comparative report by giving it a title. What about **Teachers' lives in Britain and on the planet Tharg.***? I need an opening paragraph to tell the reader what the rest of the report is about. Let me gather my ideas by looking at the grid. (See above.) What about:* **Teachers in Britain and on the Planet Tharg lead very different lives and teach different types of children.***? That sounds good.*

The first paragraph is going to be about what teachers wear. So I think I will just put a simple subheading

Clothes. *I don't need to use a subheading but I can if I want and it can help the reader. It is important I keep thinking about the reader's needs. Now what shall I tell them about the clothes. Let's look at the grid. (See above.) I know…*

Teachers in Britain are very poor and they wear jumpers and blue skirts or trousers. They do not wear much jewellery. Teachers on the planet Tharg, however, wear shiny silver tracksuits with gold helmets and orange stripes down the sides. *That's great. Hang on! What about if I change the first sentence to* ***Teachers in Britain*** *comma,* ***who are very poor*** *comma,* ***wear jumpers and blue skirts or trousers.*** *I can put that relative clause in inside commas and it sounds really good.*

Now can you make up a sentence for the next paragraph, which is all about the classrooms? Work with a partner and construct a really good sentence. Remember, we must keep all the sentences about the same thing together in the same paragraph.

Plenary

Tell the children to work with a partner to decide on the three most important things they must remember when they write their own non-chronological report. Take feedback from the children. Distribute one paper speech bubble to each pair. Tell them to select their most important point and to write it on the speech bubble with their name on it. Take the paper speech bubbles in and make a simple display on the wall with them where children can easily read them.

Taking off

Learning objectives

- To organise notes for a comparative non-chronological report.
- To draft a comparative non-chronological report.
- To consider feedback to a draft from a writing response partner and develop writing in the light of comments made, considering audience and purpose.

Resources

- Sheets C and D (pages 47 and 48)
- A selection of books, leaflets, websites and other resources about water usage

What to do

Recap on the learning in the previous session about writing a comparative non-chronological report. Together, look at the speech bubbles the children made.

Give them a copy of Sheet D (page 48) and ask them to work in groups or pairs and discuss what advice they would give to the child who wrote it.

Then get them to tell another group what they think and then discuss everyone's ideas as a whole class.

You might talk about how:
- the sentences are well constructed;
- the information is interesting;
- notes are used;
- the planning could be a bit more organised;
- paragraphs might have helped;
- subheadings could have been used;
- ideas about the same thing need to be grouped together;

- the needs of the audience should be thought about;
- the personal opinion does not help.

Remind the children that they are going to write a non-chronological report and that the audience will be reading it in a match programme. Together, consider the needs of the reader and the purpose of the report. Give the children more time to make notes if they need it.

Some children who require more support may benefit from recording their notes and ideas onto a tape recorder.

Tell the children they need to organise their notes into paragraphs so that related information is brought together.

Ask the children to look at their own comparison grids (Sheet C) and decide if they need to complete them.

Now give the children enough time to write their notes into a draft of a non-chronological report and remind them at sensible intervals to read their reports back to themselves and to share their work so far with a writing response partner, who can make suggestions and give constructive feedback.

The children who gathered notes from sources on the computer might also use the computer to make and write their grids and then write up their drafts.

Plenary

Ask the children how they feel about the planning grids. Were they useful or not? Why? Would they change them another time?

Ask them how they feel about working with a response partner who helps them to improve their writing.

Flying solo

Learning objectives

- To write a final version of a comparative non-chronological report.
- To lay out and design the double page spread for a match programme.

Resource

- Sheet E (page 49)

What to do

Once the children are satisfied that the draft they completed in the last session will meet the needs of the audience and fulfil the purpose, ask them to write their report in a final version. They could write either directly on the template on an enlarged copy of Sheet E (page 49) or on a large sheet of plain paper.

Encourage them to use pictures from the internet and other suitable publications and to write captions. They may want to illustrate the report with their own drawings.

Consider with the children appropriate types of font and use of colour and other devices of presentation, such as the use of bullet points, diagrams and charts.

They could include a text box that suggests what the reader can do now that they know about the different uses of water.

When the children have finished, give them an opportunity to evaluate each other's work. Organise them into pairs and let each one read the other's report and then write a short constructive comment, referring to criteria you agree together as a class ('*Let's make a list of the things we will be looking for in each other's reports.*')

Finally, let them design the front cover of the match programme. Ensure reference is made to water use. They could finish this for homework.

Value their writing by making a display or a small book for the library.

You could send the work to the local football club and ask them for their comments and if they would like the children to do something like this for them for real.

Guided writing

Work with the children who have been using the word processors. Give them assistance in designing the layout of the double page spread and importing pictures. Read through their reports and help them to edit their writing on screen. Discuss any differences between writing on screen and writing on paper.

Plenary

Discuss with the children what they have learned about water and about writing. Select some children to represent the class. Sit them on some chairs at the front of the classroom. Invite the headteacher to join you for this part of the plenary. Let the children tell the headteacher what they have learned about water and what they have learned about writing a non-chronological comparative report.

Comparing water use at home and in less economically developed countries

1. -

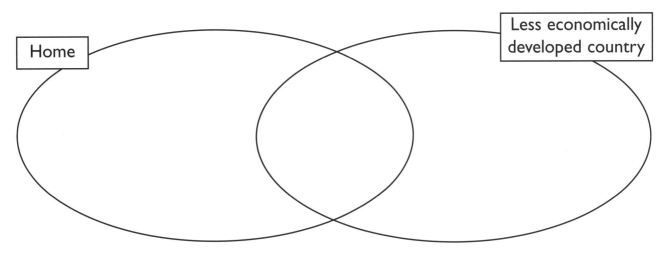

2. -

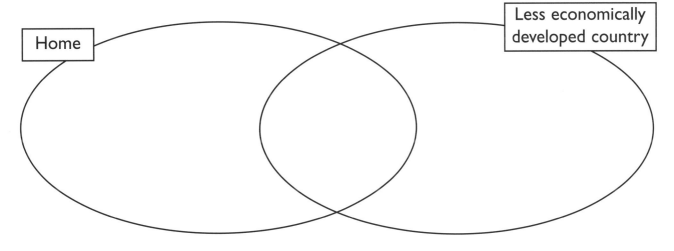

3. -

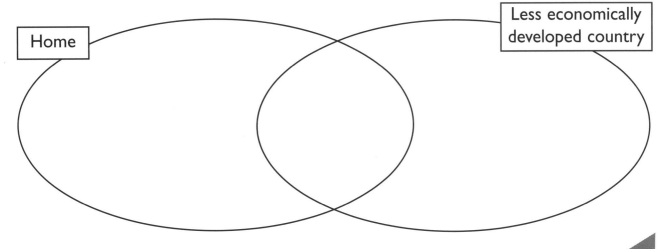

How people in less economically developed countries use water

I wake up at 5am and clean the house. I brush my teeth with twigs and by about 5.30 I go and get water from the tapstand*. It takes me 15 minutes to go and bring back one 20 litre bucket of water. I usually do this three times a day.

We use water for cooking, cleaning, drinking and washing and also for our garden to grow vegetables. I also have to use the water to clean our latrine*.

Many children throughout the world suffer greatly because they cannot easily get safe and clean water. Many children become ill with different diseases because of dirty water. They are more likely to get measles, pneumonia and diarrhoea. Diarrhoea is the second biggest killer of children under five. Because there is so little water, children cannot wash often enough and they can get diseases like scabies*, and eye infections like trachoma, which could be prevented if they could use lots of clean water. Unfortunately, many have to make do with water from dirty rivers and wells.

Often children who do not have clean water do not come to school because they are ill. They lose out on their education. We teach children the link between clean water and staying healthy but it is not easy for them and many have to make do with very little water. In the UK the average person uses 135 litres of water every day. For some people here the average is 10 litres each day. Some families even have to spend a lot of their money on buying clean water. One in six people in the world has no access to safe and affordable drinking water.

We are lucky. We have a tapstand in the village now so it is much easier to get water. Other mothers do not have it so easy. They still do not have tapstands so they must get up very early every morning and walk for miles to the nearest water hole, collect the water in containers and carry them back along the paths to their homes. They only want to make the journey once so they carry as much water on their heads or backs as possible. Often they carry 20 litres, which weighs 20kg. Oh, how my back used to ache. Before I had the tapstand there wasn't enough water to clean everything as well as I can now. Sometimes we did not have enough water to wash our hands before we ate.

*Glossary

Tapstand – a tap in a village, sometimes on a concrete pillar, which provides clean water close to people's homes
Latrine – a safe, clean and private place to go to the toilet
Scabies – a skin disease that makes people itch and is contagious; it can be caused by not having enough water to wash regularly

	Our country	Less economically developed country
How much water is used		

You might like to use some of these paragraph titles below as well as your own:

- How clean and safe the water is
- The difference water makes to education
- What people use water for
- Where people get water from

What do you think of this writing? How well does it work as a comparative non-chronological report? What advice would you give this child?

Water		
	Britain	Less economically developed country
Where it comes from	Purifying plants Taps in the house	Wells Rivers Tapstands Women carry it
What it is used for	Flushing toilets Showers Washing hands Cooking	Cooking Some cleaning Some latrines (heavy to carry so not much water at home)
Health	Water clean People healthy Some chemicals to make it clean	Polluted From rivers Animals may have been in it May have sewage in it Children get ill

The child's report – first draft

Water in less economically developed countries comes from lots of different places and ours comes from taps. Water is used to wash hands and take showers. Water can be polluted and dirty. Water in less economically developed countries can come from wells. Water in our country is used for swimming pools and it is cleaned in a big purifying plant where rubbish is removed and chemicals are added to make it clean. Water in our country and less economically developed countries is used in different ways and comes from different places. I think it must be very hard for women who have to look after children who get ill because of unclean water. Water is used for baths. Water in less economically developed countries can come from tapstands, which I think is a really good idea.

Photocopy onto A3 and fold into an A5 size leaflet.

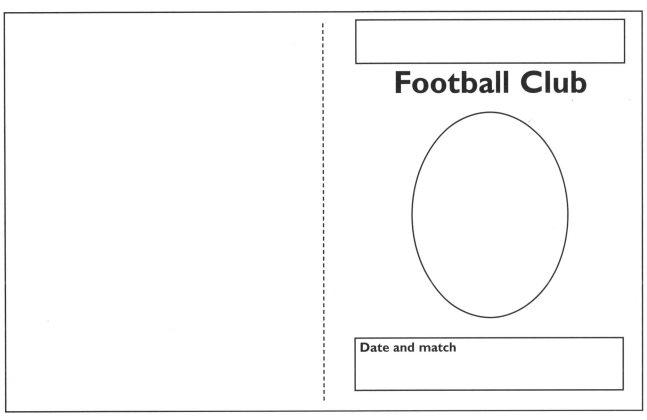

Football Club

Date and match

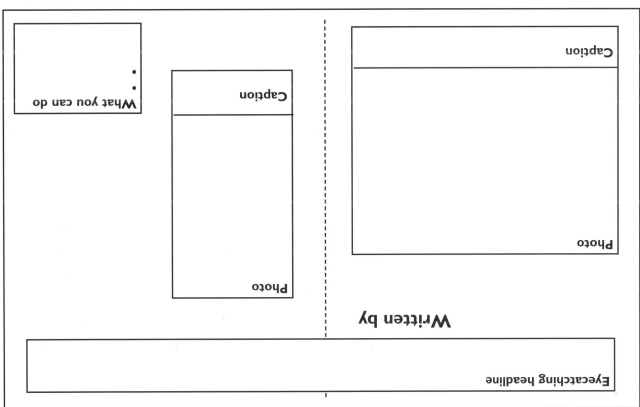

Caption

Photo

Written by

Eyecatching headline

Caption

Photo

What you can do

Chapter 3

Instruction writing

What is an instruction text?

Instructions tell someone how to do or make something. The success of the instructions can be judged by how easily the reader (or listener) can follow the procedure successfully.

Structural features

■ Heading and subheadings

■ List of items required

■ Sequence of steps to be carried out in order

■ Often has labelled diagrams

Linguistic features

■ Usually written in the imperative mood

■ Sentences begin with an imperative verb, 'you' or a time connective such as 'then', 'next', 'after that'

■ Clear and concise – no unnecessary adjectives, adverbs or 'flowery' language

Examples of instruction texts

■ recipes

■ directions

■ instructions for games

■ technical manuals

■ sewing or knitting patterns

Teaching instruction writing

One of the fundamental challenges of teaching children to write instructions is to help them consider purpose, audience and form. It is essential that they consider the prior knowledge and needs of their intended readers in order to write effective instructions that the readers can follow. Stress the importance of thinking yourself into the mind of the reader and anticipating their needs. As in writing poetry, children need to exercise some discipline in choosing just the right words and exercising economy of words so their sentences are generally simple with clear sequencing and precise language that can be easily understood by the reader. It is good to have readers using the instructions to test out the extent of the success of the writing.

While it is generally taught that instructions begin with an imperative verb, they can also begin with the word 'you' or a time connective. Children should be given freedom to judge which sort of sentence beginning is most appropriate. There is a good opportunity here to discuss the differences between the two different forms of instructional communication – speaking and listening and writing and reading – and the demands they make upon children.

Instruction writing – progression

Simple instructions are introduced in Key Stage 1 (Reception: T15; Year 1, Term 1: T13, T16; Year 2, Term 1: T13, T14, T15, T16, T17, T18).

In Year 3 children evaluate different types of instructional texts and are introduced to a range of organisational devices when writing instructions such as lists, bullet points and keys (Term 2: T12, T13, T14, T15, T16).

In Year 4 the key features of instructional texts are taught (Term 1: T22) and children learn to write instructions using linking phrases and organisational devices, such as subheadings and numbers (Term 1: T25, T26).

In **Year 5** (Term 1: T22, T25) and Year 6 (Term 3: T19, T22) children are moving on to writing and testing instructions, by revising the structure, organisational and presentational devices and language features of their instructions.

Unit 1

Lesson focus

Science Unit 5A – Keeping healthy

Overall aim

To write instructions for other children on how to prepare a healthy packed lunch, identifying some foods needed for a healthy and varied diet.

Science emphasis

The children will learn that to stay healthy we need an adequate and varied diet. They will find out why fruit and vegetables are important for a healthy diet and the possible effects of too much fat and sugar. They will apply their knowledge to producing a packed lunch that will contribute to a varied and balanced diet. This unit links to NC Sc2, 2b where children learn about the 'need for food for activity and growth, and about the importance of an adequate and varied diet for health'.

Literacy links

Year 5, Term 1: T22, T25, T26, S9

About this unit

Children and teachers meet objectives for writing instructions for the last time in the National Literacy Strategy's *Framework for Teaching* in Term 1 of Year 5. Instructions are fairly formulaic and require precision of thinking and understanding of the needs of the audience. This unit will draw upon children's prior knowledge of how to write instructions which they will have been rehearsing and developing since at least Year 1. Integrating instructions into the broader topic of 'Keeping healthy' can provide a context for this form of writing (which can be rather mundane) and allows teachers to explicitly teach the conventions of this genre of writing in a purposeful way alongside one of the most fascinating and relevant subjects for children ... food. The emphasis on instruction writing can be extended by requiring children to explain the choices for the contents of the healthy packed lunch. This can provide an additional level of challenge and interest for the children.

Switching on

Learning objective

■ To recap children's knowledge of written instructions.

Resources

■ Sheets A, B, C and D (pages 58 to 61)
■ A selection of recipes
■ Large hardback books
■ Enough cubes for each child to have 12

What to do

Organise the children into suitable mixed ability pairs and provide each pair with a large library book to act as a barrier and two dozen cubes.

Sit the children facing each other with the book positioned upright between them as a barrier. Ask one child in each pair (Partner 1) to take 12 cubes and

construct an animal without their partner seeing it. Give them a short time limit, such as one minute.

Now ask Partner 1 to give verbal instructions to their partner so that Partner 2 can construct an animal identical to the cube animal with their 12 cubes. After a specified time, say two minutes, compare the animals.

Ask the children to evaluate the quality of the instructions either between partners or in small groups and take feedback – what was it about their partner's instructions that helped and what was not so helpful? How could they be improved?

Repeat the exercise, swapping roles between the partners and then evaluate the quality of the instructions.

Now make a mind map on the board of some of the key rules of effective **verbal** instructions.

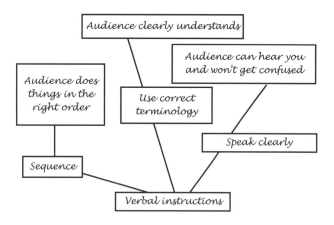

Effective verbal instructions

Sum up by stating what it takes to give effective instructions, emphasising the importance of always being aware of the intended audience for the instructions.

Now ask the children to work on dry wipe boards with a marker pen in pairs or in small groups to jot down all they can think of that will make **written** instructions effective.

Take feedback as a class and begin to construct another mind map on a large piece of paper which can be used later as a poster to remind and prompt the children while they are writing their own instructions. Write this in one colour (black) as this is going to provide a record of your assessment of their prior knowledge, which should be quite extensive. Add to it throughout the session using different colours.

Some of the things that might come up are shown in the following map.

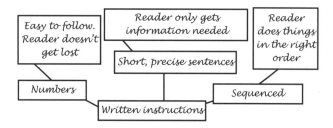

Effective written instructions

Next, tell the children that you are planning to prepare a children's party. Ask them briefly what sort of food they enjoy at a party and what they would recommend you include on your party table. Tell them you will be preparing and cooking some of the food yourself and you are going to share with them a recipe that gives instructions for making an apple crumble … one of your favourite dishes when you were a child!

Show the children an enlarged copy of Sheet B (page 59). Give them a chance to read it to themselves and then read it together, perhaps all reading aloud together, or different children reading different parts, or boys and girls taking turns to read alternate instructions.

Ask the children to discuss with the people around them whether they think it is a well written set of instructions and to give reasons for their answers. Does it include all the features of instruction texts?

Take feedback from them, perhaps designating one person from each table or group to be a spokesperson. As you respond to their comments, begin to annotate the recipe. Use Sheet A (page 58) as your prompt for the discussion. Any new features of effective written instructions can be added to the mind map.

Remind the children that often instructions begin with an imperative verb such as 'cut', 'stick' and 'bake'. These are 'doing' words. The reason is that it makes the instructions very clear and concise and is a very useful tool when writing instructions.

Divide the class into groups of six and then divide each group into three pairs. You might do this in ability groupings or it may be more suitable to have mixed ability groupings. Enlarge the three cards on Sheet C (page 60) and give each group one of each card. Each pair in the group selects one card and together the pair should read and discuss the effectiveness of the recipe card as a set of written instructions. They should make notes to annotate the recipe card in the same way you did earlier.

(Sheet D explains what is wrong with the cards on Sheet C.)

Below is how the cards should look if they are to be useful.

How to make Cornflake Crunchies	How to make Cup Cakes	How to make Jam Tarts
Ingredients 100g plain chocolate 6 tablespoons cornflakes	Ingredients 100g soft margarine 100g castor sugar 2 eggs 100g self raising flour glace cherries	Ingredients 1 packet of prepared shortcrust pastry jam
Equipment Pyrex dish Wooden spoon Saucepan Paper cake cases	Equipment Wooden spoon Mixing bowl Paper cake cases Baking tray	Equipment Board Pastry cutter Spoon Baking tray suitable for jam tarts
1. Put a small amount of water in the bottom of a saucepan. 2. Put the Pyrex dish in the saucepan. 3. Gently heat the water. 4. Melt the chocolate in the Pyrex dish, gently stirring with a wooden spoon. 5. Pour the cornflakes into the dish. 6. Stir the mixture until all the cornflakes are coated in chocolate. 7. Heap spoonfuls of the chocolate cornflake mixture into the paper cake cases and leave to cool.	1. Cream margarine and sugar together in a bowl with the wooden spoon until it goes light and fluffy. 2. Beat in the eggs one at a time, adding a tablespoon of flour with each egg. 3. Add the remaining flour, stirring gently. 4. Half fill the paper cake cases with the mixture. 5. Put the paper cake cases on a baking tray. 6. Bake in the oven for 20-25 minutes at 180C/gas mark 4. 7. When the cakes are cool, put a cherry on the top of each one.	1. Grease a baking tray suitable for jam tarts. 2. Roll out the prepared shortcrust pastry. 3. Cut circular shapes from the pastry with a pastry cutter. 4. Press each circle of pastry into a hole in the baking tray. 5. Add a little jam to each circle. 6. Put a little cold water on top of the jam. 7. Bake for 10–15 minutes in a preheated oven at 220C/gas mark 6.
Safety tip: Grown-ups should be present.	Safety tip: Grown-ups should be present.	Safety tip: Grown-ups should be present.

Set a time limit and try to focus on one group. Then tell the children to report back to the other members of their group about their recipe card. It is worth giving them a realistic amount of time to prepare what they are going to say to the other four members of their group and remind them of any speaking and listening expectations; for example:

- Speak clearly
- Wait until the other person has finished before responding and take turns speaking
- Look at each other
- Ask questions where you require any clarification

- Deal politely with any questions or opposing points of view
- Consider with respect what other people have said
- Speak in a low volume.

Enlarge the recipe cards above and display them, perhaps on an overhead projector, to show the children how the recipe instructions should look. Some useful ideas for what to point out can be found on Sheet D (page 61).

Ask the children to work in their pairs to summarise some of the things they have learned about writing instructions and then take some brief class feedback. Add anything relevant to the mind map on effective written instructions and remind the children that this mind map will provide a resource to jog their memories when they come to write their own instructions later on.

Tell them that you have put a labelled box in the classroom book corner with a selection of recipe books, children's magazines and annuals with recipes and recipe cards free from local supermarkets. Try to ensure this has a suitable selection of children's cookbooks, such as *Sticky Little Fingers* by Jane Frere (1996, Hodder Children's Books).

Plenary

Before you leave this session make connections with healthy food by asking children if they think the foods they have been focusing on today are very healthy or not and how they might fit into a healthy diet.

Tell them they will now be looking at how a varied diet can help us stay healthy.

Revving up

Learning objective

■ To extract relevant information from a range of texts about healthy eating.

Resources

■ Sheets E to H (pages 62 to 65)

■ A selection of books, leaflets, videos about healthy diets

■ Copies of leaflets from the Food Standards Agency, such as 'Enjoy Healthy Eating' (Tel: 0845 606 0667; email foodstandards@eclogistics.co.uk) and 'Just Eat

More (2003)' from the Department of Health (Tel: 020 7210 4850; *www.doh.gov.uk/fiveaday*)

What to do

Organise the children into pairs. Ask them to think of some of their favourite foods and give them a few seconds to tell each other what they are. Explain that foods provide the nutrients we need to keep healthy. We should have a variety of foods to provide all the nutrients we need to grow and keep healthy and we need to have a good balance of foods. Too much of some foods is not good for us.

Provide the children with copies of Sheet E – a survey sheet on packed lunches. Each pair should ask up to six other children what is in their packed lunch that day. You might organise for them to visit another class to ensure that there are enough people who have packed lunches to answer the questions. Instruct them how to ask questions clearly, to listen carefully and to say 'thank you' after each brief interview.

Ask if the children could put some of the empty food packaging from their lunches into a specified box at the end of lunch so that a display can be made called 'What's in our packed lunches?' This can then go on display to be referred to throughout the unit.

Discuss with the children how healthy they think the food in the packed lunches is. You could compare it with the school lunch. Raise questions as to why certain children like the sorts of food in their packed lunch. Explain that there are five different food groups:

• Bread, cereals and potatoes;
• Fruit and vegetables;
• Milk and dairy foods;
• Meat, fish and alternatives;
• Foods containing fat; foods containing sugar.
(Food Standards Agency)

Explain there are foods needed for growth and foods needed for activity as well as foods that contain large amounts of fat and sugar. Tell them the first four groups of food in the list are helpful for getting a healthy diet but the last group should not be eaten in large quantities.

Link this to any science work they have done on food and healthy eating. Educational videos and visual aids might help.

Ask the children to use the information provided in photocopiable Sheets F, G and H to make notes about healthy eating.

Spend some time talking to the class about healthy packed lunches. Ask the children to return to their class survey sheets and write comments on the quality of the foods. They might highlight those foods they think good for a healthy diet in one colour and those they think not so good in excess in another.

Plenary

Discuss with the whole class the results of their survey. Ask them to say what they have learned about healthy eating. Refer to their favourite foods and emphasise that while these are nice to have at a party, too much of this sort of food is not healthy for people.

Taking off

Learning objectives

■ To design a leaflet about healthy eating.
■ To revise the key features of instruction texts.

What to do

Discuss with the children some practical foods they could put in packed lunches that will contribute to a healthy diet, such as fruit salad, vegetable salad, pitta bread with filling, sandwiches, soup and currant buns without icing.

Tell the children that they are going to make a leaflet that gives instructions on how to prepare a healthy packed lunch. This is to be photocopied and left in the library for children and/or parents to take home. Discuss who the audience will be and how this will affect the layout and language of the leaflet. Discuss how the leaflet will look

and how it will be structured – the overall title, a brief explanation of why healthy packed lunches are important, contents of a packed lunch, instructions for preparing the packed lunch, diagrams, illustrations and safety tips. Let the children sketch their plans for their leaflets.

Tell the children that you are now going to show them how they can write the information and the instructions for their leaflets.

Demonstrate on the board part of your own instructions, reinforcing key conventions of the instruction genre. Remember to compose your sentences orally as you write and to reread after you have written, making any improvements to word choice or the word order. Justify what you write and make constant reference to the reader of your instructions.

Below is a script for your eyes only which you can use or adapt to get you going. What you write is in bold. What you say as if talking to yourself is in italics.

I need to tell the reader the reason why children need a healthy lunch.

Power-packed lunches

Growing children need a balanced, healthy and varied diet to give them the power to grow strong. Making a packed lunch full of healthy foods which will help children to grow and to stay active is not too difficult.

Hmm. I think I need to say it is fun too or readers will think it is a bit serious. **It is good FUN. Below are some instructions for ideas to make your packed lunch both healthy and yummy.**

Now I need a title and the subheadings. Then I can tell the reader exactly what he or she needs.

How to make a power-packed lunch

Equipment	Ingredients
Knife	Slice of cold cooked chicken
	Tomato
	Pitta bread
	Cucumber
	Lettuce

If I have forgotten anything I can always add it as I go along. I think my readers will be young so I had better put in a safety tip.

Safety tip: always have an adult present when you use a knife.

Now I can write the instructions in sequence and I must remember to use numbers. I will keep reading it back to myself to make sure.

What you do

Pitta Bread

1. **Take one pitta bread.**
2. **Slice it open at the top carefully with a knife (an adult may do this for you).**
3. **Put some strips of cold chicken into the bottom of the pitta bread.**
4. **Wash the tomato.**

Let's read it back. Yes. I have remembered to use imperative verbs at the beginning of each instruction and I don't think there are any unnecessary words to get in the way.

5. **Cut the tomato into small chunks.**
6. **Push the tomato into the pitta bread.**
7. **Strip some leaves from the lettuce.**
8. **Wash the lettuce leaves.**
9. **Push the lettuce leaves into the pitta bread.**
10. **Wash the cucumber.**
11. **Cut three thick slices of cucumber and neatly place at the opening of the pitta bread.**

(Note: it might be fun to make this pitta bread as you write. An assistant or other adult can help you.)

Fruit Salad

Before I move on to the fruit salad I will read it all back out loud to check it will work for the reader.

Ask the children for suggestions as to how the instructions might be written to make the fruit salad.

Plenary

Ask the children to briefly tell you the key features of an instruction text. You could display an enlarged version of Sheet A (page 58). Select some children to show their leaflet designs to the rest of the class. Invite the other children to ask questions about how the leaflet will look. Ask the selected children to predict some of the challenges they will have completing the task.

Flying solo

Learning objective

■ To write own instruction text using notes and knowledge gained from science work on keeping healthy.

Resource

■ The children's own notes about keeping healthy

What to do

Ask the children to start writing a draft of their instruction leaflet independently.

Set a time limit to get them started and some realistic expectations for different groups of children and individuals. After a defined time ask them to stop what they are doing. Allocate partners and ask them to share their work so far with their response partner. Tell them to offer advice to their partner on how the writing works and how it could be refined. They should explain to their partner how they intend to progress with their instructions so there is a sense of direction in their writing.

Let the children continue with their writing. Provide realistic time to complete the writing and periodically provide 'pit stops' where they can review each other's progress and share ideas.

Emphasise the importance of reading out loud and the value of the response partner as an audience. Remind them to use the poster of key features of instruction writing as a prompt sheet.

The children could develop their instructions to different levels of complexity and they might follow the outline below:

Must = write or word process their own instruction leaflet and illustrate it.

Should = develop the leaflet by writing some explanation of why some of the foods in their leaflet contribute to a healthy diet.

Could = compare the packed lunch and its contribution to a wider diet with children's diet in less economically developed countries.

Guided writing

When the children have made some progress with their writing, sit with one group. Present each child with a little grid like the one below:

Name of instructions writer:		
	Yes/No	Comment
Subheadings		
Numbered and sequenced		
Begins with imperative verb or time connective		
Flowery language		
All equipment listed		
Comment from reader's point of view on how reader-friendly the instructions are.		

Tell the children to swap their instructions with a response partner, read their partner's instructions and complete the grid above. Once they have written their brief comments they must share them with the writer.

Support the children as they do this and draw out all the positive points. Ensure each child is left with an idea for refinement.

Plenary

Ask the guided writing group to come to the front of the class. Ask them to reflect on how useful the response from a reader was and what difference it made to what they finally wrote. Ask them to tell you what they liked about the way other children responded to their writing and what they found unhelpful. Discuss with the children the value of response partners and the best way of giving responses to someone else's writing.

Sheet A

title to tell reader what they are going to make

How to make apple crumble

precise quantities given

Ingredients
675g cooking apples
100g plain flour
50g margarine
50g sugar

list of what is needed

Equipment
a saucepan
an ovenproof dish
kitchen scales

picture of end product

Remember to wash your hands before you start.

subheadings to guide the reader

1. Peel the apples.
2. Remove the apple cores.
3. Cut apples into wedges.
4. Place them in a saucepan with very little water and add some sugar to taste.
5. Bring to boil, cover and then simmer.
6. Stir occasionally until apples are soft.
7. Place the apples in an ovenproof dish.

numbers to help reader follow correct sequence

in time order

Making the crumble
8. Place the flour in a bowl and rub margarine into it until it resembles breadcrumbs.
9. Then add the sugar.
10. Spread the mixture evenly over the top of the apples.
11. Bake in a preheated oven at 190C/370F/gas mark 5 for about 30 minutes.
12. Finally, remove from oven with oven gloves.

imperative verb

precise language without 'flowery' or unnecessary words

Safety tip:
Make sure an adult is present. Do not handle boiling water and only use suitable knives with adult supervision. Let an adult remove your finished crumble from the oven. If in any doubt let the adult do it.

time connective

safety warning clearly emphasised

How to make apple crumble

Ingredients

675g cooking apples

100g plain flour

50g margarine

50g sugar

Equipment

a saucepan

an ovenproof dish

kitchen scales

Remember to wash your hands before you start.

1. Peel the apples.
2. Remove the apple cores.
3. Cut apples into wedges.
4. Place them in a saucepan with very little water and add some sugar to taste.
5. Bring to boil, cover and then simmer.
6. Stir occasionally until apples are soft.
7. Place the apples in an ovenproof dish.

Making the crumble

8. Place the flour in a bowl and rub margarine into it until it resembles breadcrumbs.
9. Then add the sugar.
10. Spread the mixture evenly over the top of the apples.
11. Bake in a preheated oven at 190C/370F/gas mark 5 for about 30 minutes.
12. Finally, remove from oven with oven gloves.

Safety tip:

Make sure an adult is present. Do not handle boiling water and only use suitable knives with adult supervision. Let an adult remove your finished crumble from the oven. If in any doubt let the adult do it.

Writing
across the
Curriculum

How to make Jam Tarts

Ingredients
1 packet of prepared shortcrust pastry
jam

Equipment
Board
Spoon

Grease a lovely, shiny baking tray suitable for yummy jam tarts.
Roll out the prepared shortcrust pastry.
Cut circular shapes from the roll of pastry with a pastry cutter.
Press each circle of pastry into a hole in the baking tray.
a little jam to each circle.
Put a little cold water on top of the jam.
It was baked for 10–15 minutes in a preheated oven at 220C/gas mark 6.

Safety tip:
Grown ups should be present.

How to make Cup Cakes

Ingredients
100g soft margarine
100g castor sugar
2 eggs
100g self raising flour
glacé cherries

Equipment
Wooden spoon
Mixing bowl
Paper cake cases
Baking tray

1. When the cakes are cool, put a cherry on the top of each one.
2. Bake in the oven for 20–25 minutes at 180C/gas mark 4.
3. Cream margarine and sugar together in a bowl with the wooden spoon until it goes light and fluffy.
4. Beat in the eggs that have come from a chicken one at a time, adding a tablespoon of flour with each egg.
5. Add the remaining flour, stirring gently.
6. Half fill the lovely clean paper cake cases with the mixture.
7. Put the paper cake cases on a baking tray.

Safety tip:

Ingredients
plain chocolate
tablespoons cornflakes

Put a small amount of water in the bottom of a saucepan.
Put the Pyrex dish in the saucepan.
Gently heat the water.
Melt the chocolate in the Pyrex dish, gently stirring with a wooden spoon.
Pour the cornflakes into the dish.
Stir the mixture until all the cornflakes are coated in chocolate.
Heap spoonfuls of the chocolate cornflake mixture into white paper cake cases and leave to cool.

Safety tip:
Grown-ups should be present.

Sheet D

Title missing	**Ingredients** plain chocolate tablespoons cornflakes	*Equipment missing*
Quantities of ingredients missing	Put a small amount of water in the bottom of a saucepan. Put the Pyrex dish in the saucepan. Gently heat the water. Melt the chocolate in the Pyrex dish, gently stirring with a wooden spoon. Pour the cornflakes into the dish. Stir the mixture until all the cornflakes are coated in chocolate. Heap spoonfuls of chocolate cornflake mixture into the paper cake cases and leave to cool. <u>Safety tip:</u> Grown-ups should be present.	*No numbers to make the sequence clear*

	How to make Cup Cakes **Ingredients** 100g soft margarine 100g castor sugar 2 eggs 100g self raising flour glacé cherries **Equipment** Wooden spoon Mixing bowl Paper cake cases Baking tray	
Instructions are out of sequence	1. When the cakes are cool, put a cherry on the top of each one. 2. Bake in the oven for 20–25 minutes at 180C/gas mark 4. 3. Cream margarine and sugar together in a bowl with the wooden spoon until it goes light and fluffy. 4. Beat in the eggs that have come from a chicken one at a time, adding a tablespoon of flour with each egg. 5. Add the remaining flour, stirring gently. 6. Half fill the lovely clean paper cake cases with the mixture. 7. Put the paper cake cases on a baking tray. **Safety tip:**	*Unnecessary 'flowery' language* *Safety tip missing*

	<u>**How to make Jam Tarts**</u> <u>Ingredients</u> 1 packet of prepared shortcrust pastry jam <u>Equipment</u> Board Spoon	*Some equipment missing*
Unnecessary 'flowery' language *No numbers to make the sequence clear*	Grease a lovely, shiny baking tray suitable for yummy jam tarts. Roll out the prepared shortcrust pastry. Cut circular shapes from the roll of pastry with a pastry cutter. Press each circle of pastry into a hole in the baking tray. a little jam to each circle. Put a little cold water on top of the jam. It was baked for 10-15 minutes in a preheated oven at 220C/gas mark 6. <u>Safety tip:</u> Grown ups should be present.	*A verb missing* *Slips into past tense*

Sheet E

Class survey of packed lunches

Name of child	Contents of packed lunch	Comment on how healthy the packed lunch is

The Balance of Good Health

For most people the move towards a healthy balanced diet means eating more bread, breakfast cereals, potatoes, pasta and rice, and more fruit and vegetables. Above all we should aim for variety in our food.

Fruit and vegetables

Meat, fish and alternatives

Foods containing fat; foods containing sugar

Bread, other cereals and potatoes

Milk and dairy foods

Bread, other cereals and potatoes

This group includes:

- Bread, rolls, chapattis
- Breakfast cereals, oats
- Pasta, noodles
- Rice
- Potatoes, sweet potatoes
- Dishes made from maize, millet and cornmeal
- Plantains, green bananas
- Beans and lentils

Make these foods the main part of your meals. Eat all types and choose high fibre kinds whenever you can.

Fruit and vegetables

This group includes:

- All fresh, frozen and canned fruit and vegetables.
- Salad vegetables
- Beans and lentils

Dried fruit and fruit juice can make up some of the choices from this group (see pages 19-21 for further information).

Try to eat at least five portions of fruit and vegetables each day. Include some vegetables, some salad and some fruit. Choose a wide variety.

Milk and dairy foods

This group includes:

- Milk*
- Cheese*
- Yoghurt*
- Fromage frais*

Meat, fish and alternatives

This group includes:

- Meat – beef, pork, bacon, lamb
- Meat products – sausages*, beefburgers*, meat pies
- Poultry – chicken, turkey
- Fish – fresh, frozen and canned
- Fish products – fish fingers, fish cakes
- Offal – liver, kidney
- Eggs
- Beans and lentils – baked beans, chick-peas, lentils
- Nuts and nut products such as peanut butter (see page 45 for information on food allergies)
- Textured vegetable protein and other meat alternatives

Choose a variety of foods from this group.

*Lower fat versions of these foods are available. Choose lower fat alternatives whenever you can (see pages 12-18).

Foods containing fat; foods containing sugar

This group includes:

Foods we should use sparingly, like:
- Butter
- Margarine
- Low fat spreads
- Cooking oils
- Mayonnaise and oily salad dressings

And foods we can enjoy as treats, like:
- Biscuits
- Cakes
- Puddings
- Ice-cream
- Chocolate
- Sweets
- Crisps
- Sugar
- Sweetened drinks

Try not to eat these too often and when you do, have small amounts (see pages 12-21).

Some foods such as beans and lentils fit into more than one group because of the mixture of nutrients they contain.

Eat a variety of different foods

reproduced by kind permission of the Food Standards Agency

Healthy for some

So what is malnutrition? To be healthy we need to consume appropriate amounts of energy and all the nutrients our bodies require. Too little or too much of some, over a period of months or longer may lead to ill health or malnutrition.

In simple terms, then, nutrition is about our bodies' state of health in relation to the food we eat. Malnutrition is about how our health gets damaged when we don't take in the right foods in the right balance and amount.

What do our bodies need to be healthy? The vital nutrients we need come in five groups:

- Carbohydrates provide us with energy. These are the starchy foods like bread, cereals and potatoes.

- Fats give us energy too.

- Proteins come from meat, cheese, eggs and other foods such as beans and pulses. They give our bodies the building blocks (amino acids) they need for growth and repair.

- Minerals are for growth and repair too, and they help regulate our bodies' processes.

- Vitamins are vital for some of our bodies' functions. We only need them in small amounts, but they are essential for our health.

Getting the balance

To be healthy, we need to eat the right kinds of food in the right balance. Two thirds of what we eat should be starchy foods and fruit and vegetables (at least five portions a day of these), and we should also be eating milk and dairy foods, meat, fish and alternatives, plus some food containing fat and sugar.

reproduced by kind permission of Tearfund

Sheet H

Writing across the Curriculum

Packed lunches and snacks

Trying to think of interesting and tasty packed lunches day in, day out can be difficult, especially if you're looking for healthier choices.

If your children take packed meals to school or you take them to work, try some of these ideas:

🔸 Sandwiches with thick-cut bread, rolls, crispbreads, muffins, chapattis and pitta breads with fillings such as lean meat, chicken, egg, mashed banana, cottage cheese, half-fat hard cheese, tuna, sardines, chopped raw vegetables, bean and nut spreads (see page 45 for information on food allergies).

🔸 Pasta or rice salad – for example, pasta shells, pepper, cucumber chunks, cold chopped chicken, tuna or kidney beans.

🔸 Soup, baked beans or tinned pasta in a wide-necked thermos flask with bread.

🔸 Raw vegetables such as sticks of carrot or celery, sweetcorn and salad vegetables. Or boxes of mixed chopped vegetables.

🔸 Currant buns without icing, scones or tea-breads.

🔸 Plain low fat yoghurt or low fat fromage frais with fresh fruit or fruit canned in natural juice.

🔸 Fresh fruit, such as apples, oranges, pears or peaches. Or boxes of mixed chopped fresh fruit.

All of these ideas can also make healthy snacks at any time of the day, along with:

🔸 **Pizza** made on bread rolls or scone base using half-fat hard cheese.

🔸 Sardines or baked beans on toast.

🔸 **Wholegrain breakfast cereals, which are not sugar- or honey-coated, served with skimmed or semi-skimmed milk or eaten straight from the packet.**

🔸 Plain popcorn sprinkled with paprika or Parmesan cheese.

🔸 **Roast chick-peas or sweetcorn.**

🔸 Bread sticks, wholegrain crackers, crispbreads or rice-cakes with low fat toppings or sandwich filling ideas.

🔸 **Fresh fruit.**

🔸 Unsalted nuts. (Children under five should not be given nuts due to the risk of choking. See page 45 for information on food allergies).

Take-aways and eating out

Take-away foods are often a convenient way of having a meal but many are also high in fat. If you eat them only occasionally, that is no problem, but if you eat take-away foods regularly, try to choose from these ideas:

🔸 Baked potato without butter and with low fat fillings such as cottage cheese, baked beans, ratatouille, chicken and mushroom, tuna or chilli con carne.

🔸 Ask for wholemeal buns with burgers and remember that mayonnaise can be the fattest part of the burger. Look for side salads which may be available.

🔸 Beanburger or chicken fillet in a wholemeal bun.

🔸 Sandwiches with low fat fillings.

🔸 Shish kebabs in pitta bread with salad.

🔸 Large helping of plain noodles or rice with stir-fried vegetables.

🔸 Tandoori chicken or chicken tikka with chapattis or rice.

🔸 Thick-based (deep-pan) pizza with lots of vegetables as topping.

When eating out look for cafés and restaurants displaying the **Heartbeat Award** sign in England and Wales or the **Healthy Eating Circle** sign in Northern Ireland. This

means that the catering establishment employs healthier eating practices and offers healthy food choices. It also has a non-smoking area and a very good standard of food hygiene.

It may be difficult to find healthy food choices in works' canteens.

At work, ask your catering manager, management or union to consult with the local community dietitian about how healthy your canteen food is and about offering healthier choices if necessary.

There is also an interactive website for young people giving no-nonsense facts about fast food at **www.thinkfast.co.uk**

🔸 Lunch boxes containing foods that need to be kept chilled should be stored in a fridge until they are consumed.

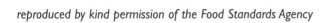

reproduced by kind permission of the Food Standards Agency

Unit 2

Lesson focus

Design and Technology Unit 5C – Moving toys

Overall aim

To write instructions for other children on how to make a toy with a cam mechanism.

Design and Technology emphasis

In this unit children will learn how to use a cam in a simple toy to control movement. They will consider the tools and materials they will use and the importance of measuring, marking out and cutting accurately. They will develop their designing skills and understanding of the working characteristics of the materials.

Literacy links

Year 5, Term 1: T22, T25, T26, S9

About this unit

This unit builds on previous D&T work done in Year 4 and leads to more complex working toys in the Year 6 Fairgrounds unit. The writing of instructions is explored in a very practical and motivating context which should grab children's attention. You will want to develop further specific design and technology skills, such as planning and handling of tools. Their understanding of written instructions will be consolidated and developed by considering the use of relevant diagrams as well as concise language suited to the needs of the audience. The children will have something to write about because they will be writing instructions for a toy with a cam mechanism that they have already made.

Switching on

Learning objectives

■ To revise the conventions of written instructions.
■ To follow instructions.
■ To know what a guider and a follower are.

Resources

■ Sheets A and B (pages 71 and 72)

What to do

The examples in this series of lessons link to work done in Year 5 on traditional stories, myths, legends and fables. Read some of these stories to the children and make a display of the books with some interesting artefacts, such as a sword or a dragon's tooth made from papier-mâché. Say that the display would be really good if there was something children and adults looking at it could touch and do. Talk about how bright and colourful working toys of some of the characters in the stories would really grab their attention. Ask them to talk to a partner and think of some of their favourite characters from the stories they have read or heard in class storytime. Take some suggestions from them.

Tell them that one of your favourite stories is about Perseus and Medusa from Greek mythology. Share an enlarged version of sheet A (page 71). Enthuse about how brave Perseus was and how he must have been terrified to approach Medusa with the hideous snakes on her head and how courageous he was to overcome his fear and slay the Gorgon.

Tell the children you are now going to show them the instructions for making a mask of Perseus's head with eyes that become terror-stricken. Ask them to recall what they already know about written instructions. They might write this down in pairs on a dry wipe board. Write some of their answers on the board – a confident child or the teaching assistant can do the writing for you as you develop the discussion.

Now show them an enlarged version of the instructions on Sheet B or give a copy to each pair. Read through the instructions with them. Explain that a 'cam' is a wheel with an axle that changes turning movements into up and down movements, a 'follower' is a piece of card or corrugated plastic that sits on the cam and a 'guider' is a piece of card that ensures the rod moves in a straight line up and down. In this model of Perseus there is no cam.

Now begin to annotate the instructions on an enlarged version of Sheet B, pointing out:

- Title to tell the reader what the instructions are for;
- Subheadings to introduce materials and tools;
- Sequenced steps with numbers;
- Diagrams to help the reader;
- Clear language;
- Begins with an imperative verb or time connective.

List these on the board and tell the children they can refer to them as a memory jogger when they come to write their own instructions for a moving toy.

Plenary

Discuss the value of the diagrams and how they help the reader. Ask them how they might improve the instructions.

Before the next session, give the children the opportunity to make the mask. After they have done this explain that you will show them how followers and guiders are really helpful when a cam mechanism is added to the moving toys and you will show them how to make one.

Revving up

Learning objectives

- To know how to make a simple cam mechanism.
- To know how to write instructions.
- To consider the needs of the audience.

Resources

- Sheets C, D and E (pages 73, 74 and 75)
- A working model of the Medusa toy made from using the instructions on Sheet C and the face on Sheet E
- A sack

What to do

Tell the children that you are now going to show them how to make a moving toy, using a cam mechanism. Remind them of the story of Perseus and his battle with Medusa. Enthuse them by talking about how frightening it must have been to encounter a woman with many snakes writhing from her scalp. Say that, just like Perseus, you have brought back Medusa's head and you have it in a sack under your chair. Bring out an old sack and untie the cords at the top. Reach inside with one hand and pretend to be bitten. Reassure the children that the Medusa's head will not turn them into stone. Now draw out from the bottom of the sack the working model of the head. Show the children the snakes moving up and down. Give them some time to enjoy and respond spontaneously. Ask if any of them know how the cardboard snakes are moving up and down.

Involve the children by turning the model around and explain that it uses a cam mechanism. Ask them to turn to a partner and explain how they think the cam mechanism was made. Give them a little time and then ask one or two of them to share their ideas with the class. Then tell them how it was made. Explain that you are going to write instructions for someone else to make the cam mechanism.

Show the children an enlarged version of Sheet D and explain that you are going to use this as a frame for writing the instructions. Ensure that there is enough space for you to write and draw on it in front of them. You might want to use an electronic smartboard. Start by writing the title and the subheadings for materials and tools, although you may want to have these already written and simply explain why they are there and move on to writing the instructions. Here is a script for you to use, starting with the first instruction. What you say out loud as if to yourself is in italics and what you write is in bold.

Now I think the first thing someone who wants to make this needs is a cardboard head to work on. So I will put a number to tell the reader that this is the first thing to do and write it really simply. Hmm. What about **It is best to cut out the shape of a head from cardboard.***? Let's read that back and see how useful it is to a reader. (Read it out again.)*

I think I need to add **strong** *so they don't use flimsy cardboard. (Insert word.) I can get rid of* **It is best to** *– that is just flowery – and start with the verb* **Cut** *so it is straight to the point. Let's read it again. (Read it out loud.) They could cut any old shape out unless I say 'Cut the shape of Medusa's head' so I'll insert* **Medusa's***. A very simple diagram of the head will help.*

Now the next instruction is a bit more complicated. Let me rehearse the sentence. I will start with a verb again. **Make two holes in a cardboard circle.** *(Read it back.) That is fine. It is accurate and precise. Now the reader needs to know where. I could write 'on either side of the centre' or 'next to the centre' or 'one above and one below the centre'. Hmm. I like the last one because even though it is a bit more wordy I think it will be very clear so I will choose this option and write it down. (Write* **one above and one below the centre***.) I think a picture will help here so I will draw something very simple. (Draw a diagram of the wheel.)*

You can continue through to instruction 4 (see Sheet C on page 73) and then reveal the remaining instructions; otherwise the children may find it difficult to concentrate for such a long time. The objective is not to write out every instruction but to demonstrate to the children what your thinking process is as you write, so they may consider and imitate it if it helps them. You could use the

wording on Sheet C for the instructions, or use your own.

Show the children the working model again and ask them if there is any way they might improve the design.

Plenary

Discuss with the children what they have learned about making a cam mechanism and what they think are some of the most important things to remember about writing instructions. Is there anything they would now add, such as safety tips?

Taking off

Learning objectives

■ To make a plan.
■ To make a simple cam mechanism.
■ To explain how they made their cam mechanism.

Resources

■ Suitable materials and equipment for making a moving toy

What to do

Tell the children that they are now going to make a moving toy linked to a traditional story, myth, legend or fable. Say that they may want to develop their cam mechanisms; for example, by using different shaped wheels or a box to house the cam. (A useful book is *Design and Technology KS2* by R Agar, 'Curriculum Focus' series, published by Scholastic Ltd.)

Give them some time to think about what to do and then let them explain it to a partner. Ask them to draw a plan of how they will make their toy. They can then share the plan with a partner and talk through it.

The children now need time to make their toy. Provide sufficient materials and tools and organise the classroom in a way that suits you. You may want the whole class to work all at once or you may want them to work in groups at different times of the day. Follow all the safety guidelines and communicate any necessary safety instructions to the children, such as concerning the use of the drill and the junior hacksaw.

When the children have finished making their toys with a cam mechanism, call them together and ask them to sit with their partners. Say that they are to give instructions to their partner about how to make their toy. Ask if they can think of any important rules for this sort of speaking and listening. Point out that you will be expecting them to:

• speak clearly;
• have appropriate volume so the listener can hear them;
• speak at a pace the listener can follow – not too slow or too fast;
• ask questions and respond to questions politely;
• look at the person they are speaking to;
• pause at points to check their partner is following and repeat anything they have not understood;
• use specific technical vocabulary, such as 'guider', not 'bit of card';
• refer to the model as a visual aid.

Plenary

Tell the children that in the next session they are going to write the instructions for making their moving toy. How might writing instructions be different from telling them? Discuss how necessary it is to have precise instructions when the audience is not there to ask for clarification. Discuss how the instructions might be set out and how important diagrams might be.

Flying solo

Learning objectives

■ To write a set of instructions.
■ To consider the needs of the audience.
■ To revise their writing after talking with a response partner.

Resources

■ Sheet D (page 74)
■ Children's own toy with a cam mechanism, made in previous lesson

What to do

Remind the children of the key features of writing instructions and briefly refer back to the instructions you modelled with them in the 'Revving up' session. Ensure a list of key features is available for every child to see.

Remind them of the spoken instructions they have given to a partner. Tell them that they are now going to write their instructions down. Remind them about the grid you used (Sheet D) in 'Revving up'. Give them their own copies of Sheet D. Ask them to quietly plan what will go in each panel in rough. Some children will feel unable to do this and want to do it neatly, so you may instead want to ask them to tell a partner what they are going to put in each cell of the grid. In this way they will have to plan but will not be tempted to spend too much time writing. This may also support those children who have difficulty with writing.

When you feel they are ready, tell the children to begin writing their instructions. Insist on quiet so that everyone can concentrate. At suitable intervals, perhaps 20 minutes, stop the whole class and ask them to read their instructions to a new partner. Tell them to give feedback, telling their partner two good things about the instructions and one thing that might need to be refined. Impress upon the children that the instructions must be understood by an audience who will follow them when the writer of the instructions is not there to answer questions, so this exercise is very important. Refer them to the list of key features of instructions. Give them sufficient time to write their instructions and bring them to a high standard of presentation. They might want to write the story their toy represents.

Make a display with the toys alongside the instructions, together with books and the children's own traditional stories, myths, legends and fables.

Guided Writing

Sit with the children who find writing more challenging. You might want to work with them individually or in pairs. Your teaching assistant will be valuable in providing the time they need for this activity. Give the children a small tape recorder each. Ask them to tell you instructions for making their toy. Ensure they are sequencing correctly and give guidance on language and quality of instruction. At each instruction ask them to say it into the tape recorder once they have rehearsed it. They can then use the tape recorder and headphones to act as their planning when they begin to write their instructions. As you listen to them recording their instructions, jot down a list of key vocabulary they will need and tape it to their desk so they can see it and refer to it as they write.

Plenary

Gather the children together and discuss what they have learned about writing instructions. Ask them to consider what the successes and challenges were, and what they found particularly difficult. Ask them what would be the five pieces of advice they would give next year's Year 5 when they come to write these instructions.

Sheet A

Writing
across the
Curriculum

Medusa the snake-haired monster

With her hair of writhing serpents, just one glimpse of the terrifying Medusa could turn you to stone

Medusa was one of three monsters called the Gorgons. They had the bodies of women, snakes for hair, teeth like the tusks of wild boars, sharp claws and wings of gold. Anyone who dared to look in the face of a Gorgon was turned to stone in horror.

The young hero Perseus was on a quest to kill Medusa. Fortunately, he had the help of the gods. Athena, the goddess of war, went with him on his journey. Hermes, messenger of the gods, gave him a sharp knife to cut off her head. Some nymphs gave him a pair of winged sandals so that he could fly, a magic helmet to make him invisible and a special pouch to keep Medusa's head in if he was successful.

One final gift was from Athena herself. She handed Perseus a shield.

"It contains no magic, but it is vital to your task," she explained.

"It's beautiful," said Perseus, admiring the gleaming shield. The bronze was so highly polished that he could see his face in it.

"Use it as a mirror," said the goddess, and the young hero understood.

Entering the place where the three Gorgons slept, Perseus squeezed through the silent crowd of stone victims. He knew that if he was to so much as glimpse Medusa's face, he too would become a lifeless statue.

He turned his face to one side and held his shield up in front of it, reflecting the sleeping Medusa in the shield's polished surface. Then, with his eyes firmly fixed on the shield, he made his way over to the sleeping form. He pulled out the knife Hermes had given him and cut off Medusa's head without ever having to look at the hideous creature.

In this way the world was rid of one more terrifying monster and Perseus earned his place among heroes.

Sheet B

How to make a mask of Perseus with moving eyes

Materials
- wooden rod
- cardboard
- cardboard mask with eye spaces cut out

Tools
- junior hacksaw
- bench hook
- glue
- ruler

1. Cut a length of wooden rod using a junior hacksaw and a bench hook. It should be a few centimetres longer than the length of your mask.

2. Cut a rectangle of card and, placing it behind the eyes of the mask, draw some terrified eyes on it.

3. Stick a small rectangle, about 5cm x 3cm, of cardboard or corrugated plastic onto one end of the rod to make a follower.

4. Stick the piece of cardboard with eyes to the other end of the wooden rod.

5. Cut some small rectangles of cardboard to make guiders.

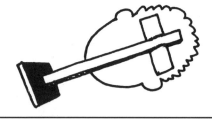

6. Lay the wooden rod on the back of the mask so that the eyes can be seen from the front.

7. Next, stick the small rectangles of cardboard over the rod onto the back of the mask to act as guiders. Make sure the rod moves freely in a straight line. Do not glue the rod to the guiders.

8. Move the eyes up and down by pushing on the follower. Paint the mask to look like Perseus.

Sheet C

How to make Medusa's head with a cam mechanism

Materials
- wooden rod
- dowel
- paper
- cardboard
- plastic tubing
- 2 cardboard or wooden wheels

Tools
- junior hacksaw
- bench hook
- drill
- glue
- ruler

1. Cut out the shape of Medusa's head from strong cardboard.

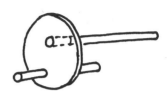

2. Make two holes in a cardboard wheel as shown above. Insert a short piece of dowel through one hole as an axle and a longer piece through the other hole as a handle. Stick the handle to the wheel.

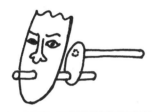

3. Make a small hole near the bottom of the mask and push the axle rod through the hole so the cam wheel is on the back of the mask.

4. Use strong glue to stick the other cardboard wheel over the end of the axle rod on the front of the mask.

5. Push the cam close to the back of the mask. Make sure you can turn it freely using the handle. Put a small length of tube on the end of the axle to keep the cam in place.

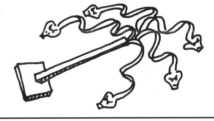

6. Cut a length of rod about half the length of the mask. Stick a small rectangle, about 5cm x 3cm, of cardboard or corrugated plastic onto one end of the rod and some paper snakes onto the other end.

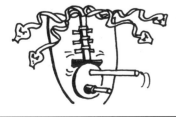

7. Lay the rod on the back of Medusa's head above the cam and stick rectangles of cardboard over it to act as guiders. Make sure the rod moves freely in a straight line. Do not glue the rod to the guiders.

8. Paint the mask. When it is dry, turn the cam wheel so the snakes move up and down.

Sheet D

1.	2.
3.	4.
5.	6.
7.	8.

Sheet E

A mask of Medusa

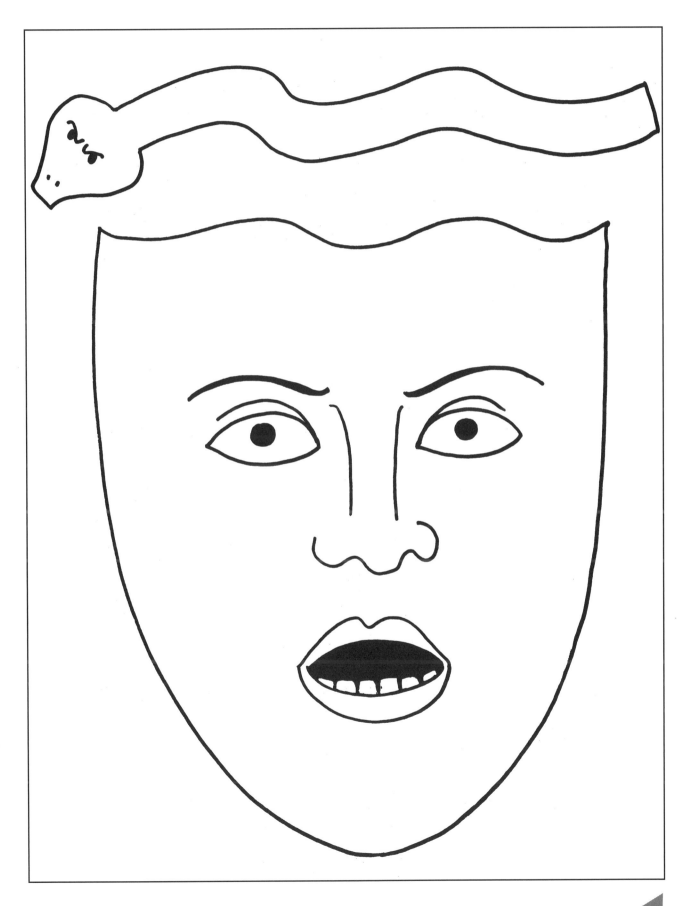

Explanation writing

What is an explanation text?

An explanation tells us how something happens or why something happens.

Structural features

- Title to tell the reader what the text will be about
- Usually has an opening statement to set the scene
- A series of logical steps explaining the process
- Often has diagrams

Examples of explanation texts

- write-ups of science experiments
- encyclopaedia entries, text books, non-fiction books

Linguistic features

- Usually present tense (except in historical explanations)
- Third person (impersonal) style
- Uses causal connectives (such as 'because', 'in order to', 'as a result of', 'consequently', 'which means that') to show cause and effect
- Use of time or sequential connectives to aid chronological order (such as 'firstly', 'afterwards', 'meanwhile', 'subsequently', 'finally')
- Often uses the passive
- Technical vocabulary
- Complex sentences

Teaching explanation writing

When children write explanations they have two main hurdles to leap. First, they have to be able to grasp the concept they are trying to explain, which requires some complex thinking skills, and then they have to articulate their understanding in the fairly rigid conventions of the written explanation genre. Plenty of opportunities to speak their explanation before writing will help children to organise their thoughts. Sharing their explanations with response partners at different stages during the writing process will give them a live audience to help them identify 'gaps' in their explanation and reveal specialised vocabulary that has not been clearly defined.

Making flow charts or simple diagrams helps to develop the children's own understanding of the process they are explaining as well as helping the reader understand the text more easily.

Explanation writing – progression

Children are introduced to explanations in Year 2 (Term 2: T17, T19, T20, T21) where they are required to read and make simple flow charts or diagrams that explain a process.

In Year 3 children develop their note taking skills Term 1: T20, T21 and Term 2: T17) into making simple records including flow charts.

In Year 4 children are introduced to the key structural and linguistic features of a range of explanation texts (Term 2: T20). They are also encouraged to improve the cohesion of their written explanations through the use of paragraphing, link phrases and organisational devices such as subheadings and numbering (Term 2: T24, T25).

In **Year 5** children are required to read a range of explanatory texts, noting features of the genre (Term 2: T15), as well as planning and writing their own explanation texts (Term 2: T22).

In Year 6 children read and write explanation texts, focusing on the use of impersonal formal language (Term 3: T15, T16).

Unit 1

Lesson focus

History Unit 13 – How has life in Britain changed since 1948?

Overall aim

To write an explanation of why it was difficult for some immigrants to settle in Britain after 1948.

History emphasis

In this unit children will learn about the reasons for and the results of a change in British life since 1948 and develop their historical understanding of the period.

Children will learn to use skills of enquiry.

Literacy links

Year 5, Term 2: T15, T16, T19, T22

About this unit

The children will develop their abilities to identify and understand 'the reasons for and the results of change'. This takes them beyond a straightforward description or even a comparative report and challenges them to think at a deeper level, to use their research to make links and develop explanations for a social change since 1948. Underpinning this unit are skills of enquiry and the teacher needs to demonstrate how to ask questions to focus research, select and combine information from different sources and articulate the facts and their explanations in a written form.

The children will undertake an enquiry in small groups and the teacher needs to demonstrate the process to do this successfully. There are valuable opportunities for explicit teaching and reinforcing of speaking and listening skills.

Switching on

Learning objective

■ To understand the key features of an explanation text.

Resources

■ Sheets A and B (pages 82 and 83)
■ A suitcase with various items needed for a long trip
■ Atlases
■ Books and photographs of life in the Caribbean

What to do

Tell the children you are going on a long journey and you need to take with you everything that is important. Ask them what you might need to take. Begin with simple things like toothbrush and towel, produce them from a pile you have already prepared and put them into the suitcase. Then talk about your clothes and tell them it will be a hard choice which to take and which to leave as you can't carry everything. Put your favourite clothes into the suitcase. Move on to other possessions such as photo albums, CDs and special souvenirs and discuss why you will take some and not others. (You might put a class

photo in your suitcase.) Begin to talk about how you feel about leaving friends and family and your excitement and fears about going somewhere far away where you have never been before.

Ask the children if they have ever been to a new place. Encourage them to talk about moving house or starting a new school or even any holidays they might have had. Discuss with them their experiences; for example, not knowing anyone, not knowing what to do at the table and being confused and lost in a building. Ask them to try to describe how they felt or how they think it would feel.

Tell them that they are going to learn about some people who came to Britain from some islands far away in the Caribbean shortly after World War II. Give them an atlas and ask them to find the Caribbean islands. Show them some pictures of places in the Caribbean. Consider how far the islands are from Britain and how long it might have taken people to get to Britain in a boat.

Point out to the children that there were many reasons for people from the Caribbean wanting to come to live in Britain after the war. Can they think of any? Perhaps some children may have relatives or friends who actually made the journey and will offer some insights.

Tell the children that you have a text that explains why people left the Caribbean in 1948. Show them an enlarged copy of the text on Sheet B (page 83). Say that the purpose of reading this text is to find out why immigrants came to Britain. You might ask them to read it quietly to themselves before it is read aloud.

Discuss some of the reasons people emigrated from the Caribbean and then ask the children to get into small groups to construct a short drama. Tell them that each person in the group is to pretend to be one of the immigrants, except one child who is to pretend to be a relative trying to persuade them to stay in the Caribbean. Give the children some time to discuss their roles and think what to say. You might gather together all the children playing the relative and make up some arguments they can use to persuade the others in the group to stay. Give the children sufficient time to complete their drama. Take feedback from the class about some of the reasons they gave for emigrating and how they felt.

Tell the children they are going to write their own explanation of what happened when the emigrants arrived in Britain but first they are going to find out what the key features of an explanation text are. Return to the text on Sheet B. Using Sheet A as your prompt, annotate the text and emphasise and explain all the key features of an explanation text. Make a list of the key features and display it where all the children can refer to it later.

Plenary

Ask the children to reflect on how the emigrants from the Caribbean would have felt. Discuss what they think they would feel like when they arrived in Britain after their boat journey from the Caribbean. You might want to read a short section from Floella Benjamin's excellent book *Coming Home*.

Revving up

Learning objectives

■ To identify what they already know about why people came to Britain from the Caribbean after World War II and develop questions to prepare for research.

■ To make notes.

■ To make a plan for explanation writing.

Resources

■ Sheets C and D (pages 84 and 85)

■ Highlighting pens

What to do

Explain to the children that next they are going to find out what happened to their characters from the drama in the 'Switching on' session when they arrived in Britain after their journey. Ask them to discuss in pairs what they already know and what questions they may have. Take feedback from the class and write the questions on the board. Now discuss what sort of challenges the people might have had to face (weather, finding somewhere to live, school, food).

Tell the children they will need to use different sources to find the answers to their questions. These might be the internet, CD-Roms and reference books. Sheet C is another resource they can use. It contains statements from people who were immigrants in the 1950s.

Tell the children that later on they are going to do their own piece of writing explaining why the immigrants found it difficult at first to settle in Britain. Say that first they are going to make some notes by highlighting the following in the text on Sheet C: three major reasons for difficulties in one colour and three other reasons in another colour (they can use pale coloured crayons if highlighters are not available). Ask them to do this in pairs and, while they are working, target some children to support and extend. You might ask the more able to use other texts you have collected and made available to supplement their notes.

When they have finished highlighting, ask the children to list their points on a separate piece of paper. Then bring the class together again, take feedback on their major findings and address any misconceptions.

Next, ask the children to get back into their drama groups. Choose one from each group to pretend to be the relative who visits the other immigrants in Britain. Tell them that the relative must hotseat the other children about the problems they faced when they arrived in Britain.

Show the children how to collect and organise information and begin to plan reasons for their own explanation text, using an enlarged version of the planning tree on Sheet D; for example:

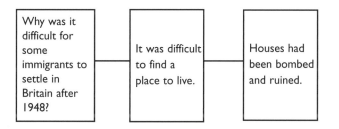

Why was it difficult for some immigrants to settle in Britain after 1948?	It was difficult to find a place to live.	Houses had been bombed and ruined.

Then give them their own copies of Sheet D and let them finish it in pairs.

Plenary

Choose two or three children to be hotseated by the rest of the class about the problems they faced when they arrived in Britain. Discuss with the children their feelings about this.

Taking off

Learning objectives

- ■ To use a plan.
- ■ To begin writing an explanation text.

What to do

Tell the children that you are going to do some shared writing of an explanation, using the notes and the planning tree made in the previous session. Discuss who the audience might be and how you might publish their writing so others can read it; for example, a display board in the library or a class book that can be loaned to other classes in the school.

Refer to the list of key structural and linguistic features you previously made to model how to remind yourself of the particular 'shape' of an explanation.

Now say to the children, 'I am going to write a few sentences and you are going to watch.'

Start to write in front of them, remembering to model gathering your ideas, rehearsing the sentence and reading it back, paying attention to vocabulary choice and perhaps changing some vocabulary and word order. It is important to actually refer to these so as to positively model how to use planning and notes. It is best only to do a few sentences before involving the children directly.

Following is a script **for your eyes only** which you can use or adapt. The text in italics is what you say out loud as if to yourself; the text in bold is what you write.

I need a title that indicates to the reader what the explanation is going to be about. Let's write **Why was it difficult for some immigrants to settle in Britain after 1948?** *and remember to put the question mark on*

it. Now I need a short paragraph that is like a doorway and sets the scene before I go into detail. A sentence will do. I want to say something about people from the Caribbean coming a long way and what surprised them. What about:
After their long journey across the Atlantic there were some surprises for the Caribbean immigrants and life was not always what they had expected.?

I'll just read that back. I think I need to add in words that tell the reader they were coming to Britain, so I will just insert 'in Britain'. Now let's read it back.

After their long journey across the Atlantic there were some surprises for the Caribbean immigrants and life in Britain was not always what they had expected.

Now let me look at my plan for my next paragraph. It is going to be about the difficulty finding somewhere to live. Explanations are about giving reasons for things, so a good way to start the paragraph is to write 'One reason for...'
So what about: **One reason for this was that it was difficult to find somewhere to live.?**

Let me read it all back to myself. It sounds really good. Now I need to say why it was difficult to find somewhere to live. Let me look at the notes. Can you make up a sentence with a partner that would tell the reader why it was difficult?

Give the children time to work in pairs to make up the sentence orally or to write it as well on a dry wipe board. Ask the pairs to read their sentence to another pair because often when children read their writing aloud they can hear and see areas for improvement, such as words missed out.

Let me use some of your sentences to finish off this paragraph. (Read from some of the whiteboards, making changes where necessary, and saying why you choose to use these sentences. Then read them back.)

Let's see what it sounds like now. I will read it back to you.

This was because a lot of the housing had been destroyed during the war. Often men would share rooms and have to share the cooker, so it was difficult to prepare meals. Often they were charged a lot of money for rent because some landlords were mean and crooked. Some people refused to rent rooms to immigrants.

What do you think? Does it work?

Some children with specific learning difficulties may find it difficult to read from the board as you write and it is worth considering how to accommodate their needs. Perhaps choosing certain colours of pen or flip chart paper may help. You may want to number the lines. It may be helpful to use different colours for different sentences or paragraphs.

Ask the children to begin writing their own introduction and first paragraph. Then ask them to sit with a response partner to share what they have written.

First, discuss how they might support each other when they are working as response partners and discussing each other's writing. Tell them some of the things they can ask their partner are:

- Did you have any other problems? (Look at the planning tree.)
- Listen to your sentence; does it works?
- Can you pack the reason into the sentence using a connective like 'because' or 'so'?
- Can you see a way of putting the connective at the front of the sentence?

Plenary

Choose two or three children to read out their explanations so far. Ask them to identify how their response partner helped them to improve their writing. Invite the class to finish the sentence 'A really good response partner...' Tell them they should try to do the things they have just suggested.

Flying solo

Learning objective

■ To write an explanation text.

Resources

■ Sheet E (page 86)

■ The children's own introduction and first paragraph from the previous session

What to do

Tell the children you want them to complete their own explanation, using the notes and list of key structural and linguistic features to guide them. Set small targets for some groups. Remind them of any personal targets (for example, to use a complex sentence). Stop them after a suitable time (say 15 minutes) and ask them to read through their work so far, making sure it reads well. They could work with a partner to do this. Remind them of the suggestions for working with a response partner discussed in the last session. Once they have reviewed their writing so far, ask them to continue.

Some children may use a writing frame such as the one on Sheet E (page 86).

After, say, ten minutes, gather the class together to discuss how to write a conclusion for their explanation. Tell them that a concluding paragraph in an explanation needs to:

• briefly sum up the reasons given during the explanation;

• give a short answer to the question set at the beginning – often in the title.

Now model writing your own conclusion in front of the children. You can use or adapt the example below:

Settling in Britain after 1948 was difficult for some immigrants for several reasons. Sometimes they were not treated fairly. Some people found it cold and expensive to live and some children found it hard to settle into a new school.

Plenary

Choose some children to read out their explanations to the class. Photocopy them onto OHTs and show them to the class as they are read out. Ask the children to respond in a positive way to the writing. Ask the authors of the chosen explanations if there is anything they would do again or do differently next time they write an explanation. Now ask the other children to turn to a partner and reflect on the same question.

Writing
across the
Curriculum

title
telling the
reader what the
question is

general
statement
to set the scene
before getting
into detail

Why did immigrants come to Britain from the Caribbean after 1948?

Immigrants made the journey from the Caribbean to live and work in Britain after 1948 for a variety of reasons.

After the war there was a lot of work to be done in Britain to rebuild the country. A lot of men were needed and there were not enough to do all the jobs. In order to fill all the vacancies, companies like London Transport and hotels put advertisements in Caribbean newspapers asking men to travel to Britain to work. Many responded.

causal
connective

Caribbean men were happy to work in Britain because jobs in the Caribbean were not very good and there was high unemployment. Many men used to work harvesting bananas and sugar, which was seasonal work and poorly paid, or they had to work in Florida and Panama. Britain seemed to offer better jobs and more money.

reasons
given in a
logical order

Some people wanted a better life for their children and they thought that working in Britain would offer a better education and more money, so they made the long journey to Britain.

Another reason men were willing to live in Britain was that they had already been living in Britain during the war as a result of serving in the Royal Air Force or other armed services, so they knew what Britain was like and liked it.

past tense
and third
person

A further reason was that the Caribbean was part of the British Empire, which meant that the people born there had a right to live in Britain. Many Caribbean people saw themselves as closely linked to Britain and were happy to go to what was once considered their mother country.

Finally, people were able to travel across the ocean from the Caribbean because after the war many ships were taking people back to the parts of the world they had come from before the fighting. Many of the ships stopped in the Caribbean and people were able to pay the cheaper fare.

complex
sentence

Caribbean people came to Britain because they were invited to help rebuild the country and they thought they would find a better life for themselves and their families.

brief
conclusion
to summarise

Why did immigrants come to Britain from the Caribbean after 1948?

Immigrants made the journey from the Caribbean to live and work in Britain after 1948 for a variety of reasons.

After the war there was a lot of work to be done in Britain to rebuild the country. A lot of men were needed and there were not enough to do all the jobs. In order to fill all the vacancies, companies like London Transport and hotels put advertisements in Caribbean newspapers asking men to travel to Britain to work. Many responded.

Caribbean men were happy to work in Britain because jobs in the Caribbean were not very good and there was high unemployment. Many men used to work harvesting bananas and sugar, which was seasonal work and poorly paid, or they had to work in Florida and Panama. Britain seemed to offer better jobs and more money.

Some people wanted a better life for their children and they thought that working in Britain would offer a better education and more money, so they made the long journey to Britain.

Another reason men were willing to live in Britain was that they had already been living in Britain during the war as a result of serving in the Royal Air Force or other armed services, so they knew what Britain was like and liked it.

A further reason was that the Caribbean was part of the British Empire, which meant that the people born there had a right to live in Britain. Many Caribbean people saw themselves as closely linked to Britain and were happy to go to what was once considered their mother country.

Finally, people were able to travel across the ocean from the Caribbean because after the war many ships were taking people back to the parts of the world they had come from before the fighting. Many of the ships stopped in the Caribbean and people were able to pay the cheaper fare.

Caribbean people came to Britain because they were invited to help rebuild the country and they thought they would find a better life for themselves and their families.

Sheet C

Reasons for some immigrants finding it difficult to settle in Britain after 1948

**Interviews for a local
radio programme with
people who were
immigrants from the
Caribbean in the 1950s**

What do you remember
about arriving in Britain in
the 1950's ?

Most of all I remember how excited I was but it was cold. Oh, so cold. We had been told Britain was cold but I really felt it and during winter – well – I used to be so sad and long for the sunshine. Especially if it was foggy too. But I was young and my heart was always full of springtime.

I was a young man then and I didn't mind so much sharing a room with other men. It was all I could find at first and it wasn't cheap, I can tell you. It wasn't always easy trying to share a single cooker with the others, especially after a hard day's work but we got along pretty well. I enjoyed watching the football and some of us would go together to the local game on a Saturday.

Well, I remember how expensive I thought it was to rent a room. But there wasn't much to choose from, what with so many houses being bombed during the war and so many new houses needing to be built. But we had some good friends and that made things better.

I remember our landlord was fair. We were lucky. Some of the landlords near us were – well – they were crooked and used to charge my friends far too much money and those landlords didn't bother to look after the houses or the people living in them. That I didn't like, but, you know, there wasn't too much choice for us at first.

I loved my books but I was a bit surprised when I arrived at my new school and the teacher put me in the bottom group. She didn't even bother to test me. Still, I worked hard and I was okay but I know some of the children lost heart and didn't bother to try after a while because some of the teachers, they didn't really understand the way we felt. Sometimes we were teased by the other children because of our accents. I was the only black person in my school for a long time and sometimes it was a bit lonely, I can tell you.

My parents loved to go to church and we had to go, every week, to the local Pentecostal church. Everyone was singing and we had a lot of fun there. There were lots of Caribbeans and I guess my mum and dad felt at home there.

Sheet D

Planning tree

Reason **Supporting fact 1** **Supporting fact 2**

Why/How …

Why was it
difficult for
some
immigrants to
settle in Britain
after 1948?

Writing frame

<table>
<tr><td colspan="1">Why/How…</td></tr>
</table>

After 1948 immigrants arriving in Britain…
One reason for this…
Because…
Another reason they…
Settling in Britain was…

Remember:
Start with a general statement.
Give sequence of reasons.
Sum up at the end.

Use some of these connectives: because, in order to, so, as a result of, then, consequently, therefore, which meant that.

Unit 2

Lesson focus

Science Unit 5E – Earth, Sun and Moon.

Overall aim

To write an explanation of how day and night are related to the spin of the Earth on its own axis.

Science emphasis

This unit develops children's ability to use and apply scientific knowledge to phenomena that surround them. It encourages them to use scientific evidence about the Earth, Sun and Moon to explain why the Sun seems to move across the sky and articulate that it is because the Earth spins on its own axis once every 24 hours. The children are to understand how day and night are related to this spin.

Literacy links

Year 5, Term 2: T15, T16, T22, S6

About this unit

This unit follows on from work done with children where they will have learned about the relative sizes of the Earth, Sun and Moon and that they are all spherical. They will have done experiments with shadow sticks or drawing around their own shadows at different times of the day to reveal how the Sun appears to move across the sky.

It may also build on work previously done on the changes in the appearance of the Moon.

Switching on

Learning objective

■ To understand the features of an explanation text.

Resources

■ Sheets A, B and C (pages 93 to 95)

What to do

Take the children into an area that has a lot of space, such as the hall or playground. Tell them that you are going to explain how the Moon appears to change its shape. (Use the diagrams on Sheet B to help you.) Involve the children in a demonstration as suggested in Science SoW Unit 5E, Earth, Sun and Moon. Ask a group of them to stand together to represent the Earth. Ask another child to walk round the group to represent the Moon. As he or she walks round the group they should always face them as the Moon always faces the Earth.

Back in the classroom explain to the children how the Moon changes shape (use Sheet B to help you). The reason for doing this is to compare a verbal explanation with a written one later on. You may want to use the following script to get you started:

You know the Moon has got a different shape each night, right? That's because the Moon is, er, the Moon is moving around the Earth all the time, right? So, when it's on the other side of the Earth from the Sun, opposite the Sun with the Earth in the middle, yeah, there's a full moon. That's because the whole of one half of the Moon is being lit up by the Sun and we can see all of this half reflecting light from the Sun. So, the next thing is, when the Moon moves to one side of the Earth, the right of the Earth, you only see a smaller part of it because you can only see part of the reflection. Right? So the light on the Moon is from the Sun. When the Moon is in front of the Earth, between the Earth and the Sun, you can't see any of it because the Sun is reflecting on the front part of the Moon and you can't see the Moon because it is the back of it that is facing the Earth and there is no light hitting it. Right? Got it so far? Okay. Then the Moon moves round to the left of the Earth and you can only see a smaller part of it again. And so on. Any questions?

On a flip chart or board draw a comparative grid with two columns. Write the heading 'Skills when **speaking** an explanation' at the top of one column and 'Skills when **writing** an explanation' at the top of the other.

Discuss with the children the different things you had to think about while you were giving your oral explanation. List all the techniques that were used in the grid.

Skills when **speaking** an explanation	Skills when **writing** an explanation
• considering what the audience already knew • choosing vocabulary • tone of voice • volume • eye contact • checking they follow the explanation at different points • listening to questions and answering questions • changing pace • not repeating yourself	

Now ask the children what they know about a written explanation text and how they think it might be different from a spoken explanation.

Enlarge Sheet B so that all the children can see it or make a copy for each child. Tell them that this is the same explanation of how the Moon appears to change shape that you have just been explaining to them. Now they can see it in a written form. Read it through with them, referring to the diagrams as you go.

Some children with specific learning difficulties may find reading this amount of text very challenging. One way of helping them is to give a copy of the text to a teaching assistant before the lesson to read through with the child. This kind of support before the whole class reads together might prepare the child and enable him or her to take a more active part in the shared reading part of the lesson.

It is quite a complicated concept so you may want to reinforce the children's understanding with some objects such as a football, tennis ball, table tennis ball and a torch.

Identify and discuss with the children the key structural and linguistic features of an explanation text, using the

annotations on Sheet A (page 93) to guide you. You may want to highlight and annotate the shared explanation as you do this. You could also insert subheadings above some of the paragraphs if this helps your children.

Plenary

Discuss with the children how writing an explanation requires different skills from speaking an explanation. Ask them to work in pairs to think of three differences. After a few minutes, stop the children and listen to their feedback. Add their ideas to the list on the comparative grid on the flip chart or board. It may look like this:

Skills when **speaking** an explanation	Skills when **writing** an explanation
• considering what the audience already knew • choosing vocabulary • tone of voice • volume • eye contact • checking they follow the explanation at different points • listening to questions and answering questions • changing pace • not repeating yourself	• can't ask audience if they follow, so need to read back and ask a partner • must use complete sentences that make sense • must check the sequence of process is right • structure is very strict

Tell the children that they can add to this as they find out new things during the rest of their work on explanations.

Revving up

Learning objectives

■ To consider the needs of an audience for writing.

■ To visually map information.

■ To make notes in preparation for oral and written explanation.

■ To develop speaking and listening skills.

Resources

■ Sheet C (page 95)

■ A tape recording of the myth on Sheet C (optional)

■ A tape recorder

What to do

Find an official-looking brown envelope and write the name of your class and the school address on the front. Place inside it a photocopy of the letter from the Ministry of Exploration (Sheet C). If you can, make a tape recording of the children's myth about how day and night occur that is written on Sheet C, perhaps disguising your voice or enlisting the help of a willing friend to make the recording. Put it in the envelope and seal it.

Ask the school secretary to bring the envelope into your classroom in an ostentatious manner just as you are ready to begin the lesson. Tell the children the envelope has just arrived by special delivery. Make a big fuss, read the letter and play the tape once or twice to the class.

If you wanted to develop this further, you could arrange for the teaching assistant or a willing colleague or parent to dress up as a parent from the island and let the children in your class hotseat them. You may even enlist some children from Year 6 to pretend to be children from the island.

Now put the children into groups of four. Give them a copy of the letter and tell them to write down all they know about how day and night happen – visual maps might help them to develop and record their thoughts.

Before they start, make clear your expectations of how they should go about their discussion. For example:

• allocating roles;
• listening carefully to each other;
• building on one another's contributions;
• being polite;
• valuing each other's ideas;
• speaking no louder than is necessary for the others to hear.

Give one child in each group the task of reporting back on how well the other children met these speaking and listening expectations. Give them adequate time to do this task and expect a level of working noise.

Bring the groups together with their notes. Briefly draw together their understanding of how night and day occur and ensure that there is an accurate and shared understanding of how day and night are related to the spin of the Earth on its own axis. Draw a class flow chart to help them.

Now send the children back to their groups to briefly discuss how they might explain this to the children from the island. Again, remind them of your expectations for oral work in groups. Praise them for everything they have done well in the previous group work.

Plenary

Bring the children back together. Arrange for a colleague or children from Year 6 to pretend to be adults or children from the island. If this is not possible, select some children from your class to pretend, with you, to be adults and children from the island. Invite one or two children to explain to the island people how day and night occur. This might provide a good opportunity for higher achievers to use their speaking and listening strengths.

Reflect with the class afterwards on their experience of explaining. Did they use any of the skills on the comparative grid you made earlier? Is there anything else to add?

If possible, ask the island people to give their opinions on the explanations.

Taking off

Learning objectives

■ To plan and present an oral explanation.

■ To deliver an oral explanation and reflect on strengths and areas for development.

Resources

■ Sheet D (page 96)

■ A selection of information texts about night and day

What to do

Recap on the work that was done in the previous session and tell the children they will be working in small groups.

Tell them that their task is to explain verbally to the island children how day and night occur, using their scientific knowledge. Remind them of what was discussed in the plenary of the previous session about the skills needed to complete this task successfully.

Tell them that their spoken explanation must last no longer than three minutes and they should use visual aids or drama if appropriate.

Remind them of your expectations for working in groups and tell them you will be feeding back to the groups on their speaking and listening skills.

Show them how to use their planning sheet (Sheet D) to guide them and make sure each group has at least one enlarged copy.

Make available an adequate selection of supporting information texts from the school library.

Spend time observing each group and make succinct notes about their speaking and listening skills based on

the guidance given to them earlier. You can use these to feed back to them later and they can contribute to your own record keeping.

Give the children adequate time to complete the task.

Establish a way of giving them time and space to actually make their oral presentations. There are several options to meet the children's needs and restrictions of time and space management.

• Throughout the day, groups go out of the classroom to a designated area with a teaching assistant or parent and **each child** gives the oral explanation the group have created into a video camera.

• Groups give an oral explanation to the whole class and the performance is evaluated afterwards. This oral explanation could be recorded on video.

• In subsequent days groups could work with you in guided speaking and listening sessions. You could watch children's oral explanations and together discuss and evaluate their presentations.

Plenary

Select some children to tell the other children what some of the successes and challenges were when they worked in groups and what they have learned about working in groups and making oral presentations. Tell them that they will be able to use what they have learned next time they have to do something similar.

Flying solo

Learning objectives

- To write an explanation.
- To use a visual resource to support writing of an explanation.
- To consider differences between writing and orally presenting an explanation.

Resources

- Sheets B and E (pages 94 and 97)
- split pins
- scissors

What to do

Tell the children that the island children require a permanent record of an explanation of how night and day occur.

Together reread the explanation of how the Moon appears to change its shape (Sheet B) and remind the children of the key conventions of explanation writing. Make a list of the key things they must remember and display it where they can all see it. For example:

- opening sentence to introduce topic;
- causal connectives, such as 'because', 'as a result';
- present tense;
- separate paragraphs for different parts of the explanation;
- closing statement.

Demonstrate for the children how to write the first part of the explanation of how night and day occur and why the Moon appears to vanish during the day. Remember to talk aloud as you write, explaining your choices of words and sentences. Emphasise to the children the importance

of frequently reading back with the eye of the reader as you write so the explanation hangs together in a logical structure and all the questions the reader may have are answered with clarity.

The following script may be useful. It is for your eyes only and you can use it or adapt it. The text in italics is what you say out loud as if to yourself; the text in bold is what you write.

I need to introduce my explanation with a title that makes sure the reader knows what the explanation is about. I could just write 'Night and Day' but I think it's too vague. I ought to use the words 'How' or 'Why' because that is what explanations are about, so I think… **How are day and night caused?**

Now I need a sentence that will introduce the explanation to the reader. A lot of science is about observing what happens and then explaining it, so I am just going to say in the first sentence what we observe. Let me think to myself for a moment. Now I can say the sentence out loud. This helps me to hear what my sentence is going to sound like to the readers – the island children. What about: **Part of every day we live in the light and the Sun appears to hang in the sky. Part of every day we live in the dark and the Sun seems to disappear.***?*

I think because we know our audience we could add a little sentence to reassure them. What about: **At the end of every night the Sun comes back.***?*

Let's read this back. Hmm. What about replacing comes back with 'reappears'?

What do you think? Let's change it.

At the end of every night the Sun reappears.

If I read the whole paragraph back I can check it is in the present tense and all the punctuation is correct. (Read it back.)

I think that will introduce the explanation. Now, how shall I start my next paragraph? (Let the children make suggestions.)

Tell the children they should use some form of diagram to support their written explanation. Show them how to make the rotating Earth and Sun (Sheet E). Ask them if they can think of any way of improving the diagram to make it easier to understand. Explain that if they want to they should make and use their own visual aid.

Send the children off to write their own explanation and give them time to complete it. Some of them might use the computer.

They might use the notes they made for the oral explanation or they might want to gather some new information, so make sure some reference material from the library is available.

Set small targets for some groups. Remind them of any personal targets. Stop them at intervals and give them opportunities to read and respond to each other's work and make any adjustments to their own writing in the light of comments made.

Guided writing

Select a middle ability group. Write a short list of 'gluing words' (causal connectives) for explanations with them on a dry wipe board. Remind them that these are words and phrases that relate to time and cause, such as 'because', 'as a result', 'this means' and 'when this happens'. Tell them these words will help them to express themselves clearly and tie their ideas together. Spend some time helping them to read their sentences to each other and encourage them to refine their sentences by using these gluing words. Praise their work so far and highlight where they have used words and phrases which relate to time and cause.

Plenary

Recall the children together. Perhaps just one or two of them can read out their written explanation. Now spend some time evaluating the different challenges they met and skills they needed when writing an explanation to those they met and needed when giving an oral explanation. Consider together what they have learned about writing and how the knowledge might be used the next time they write.

Sheet A

opening sentence to introduce topic

title to introduce what is to be explained

How does the Moon appear to change its shape?

When people look at the Moon at night it seems to have its own light. It appears to change shape, and sometimes to disappear altogether.

Even though it does seem to be like a giant light bulb in the sky, the Moon has no light of its own. All the light of the solar system comes from the Sun, so when we look at the Moon what we are really seeing is the reflection of the Sun's light which has hit the Moon and is reflecting back to us.

first person – suits this explanation but it is mostly in third person

present tense

The Moon is always in our skies, day and night. It travels all the way round the Earth and takes 28 days to make the whole journey. This is called 'orbiting the Earth'. While it is orbiting the Earth it rotates once on its own axis. This is why, as it is moving around the Earth in a circle, the same half of the Moon faces the Earth at all times (Diagram A).

As the Moon orbits the Earth, sometimes it is between the Sun and the Earth and at other times it is further away from the Sun than the Earth is (Diagram A).

separate paragraphs for different parts of the explanation

When the Moon is directly between the Sun and the Earth, although it is still there, it cannot be seen at night because we cannot see any of the side that is lit up. When this happens we call it the 'new moon'. The sky is black and the Moon is invisible (Diagram A).

When the Moon is on the other side of the Earth, in line with the Sun, then we are able to see all of the side facing the Earth. It looks like a great big white shining disc because light is reflecting from the whole of the Moon's surface which is facing the Earth. This is called a 'full moon'. The other side of the Moon is of course in darkness (Diagram B).

time connective to aid progression of the sequence

causal connective

It takes around 14 days to move from full moon to new moon. During this journey, the same part of the Moon is facing the Earth, but less and less of this side of the Moon is being lit by the Sun. As a result, the Moon appears to get smaller each night and changes its shape until it disappears altogether when it reaches the new moon position.

Of course, the same thing happens during the next 14 days except that the Moon appears to grow as it moves back towards the full moon position.

closing statement

The Moon is always there, a rotating ball of rock. It never changes. It is the light and the movement that make it seem to change.

How does the Moon appear to change its shape?

When people look at the Moon at night it seems to have its own light. It appears to change shape, and sometimes to disappear altogether.

Even though it does seem to be like a giant light bulb in the sky, the Moon has no light of its own. All the light of the solar system comes from the Sun, so when we look at the Moon what we are really seeing is the reflection of the Sun's light which has hit the Moon and is reflecting back to us.

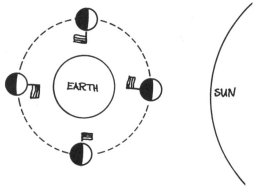

Diagram A

The Moon is always in our skies, day and night. It travels all the way round the Earth and takes 28 days to make the whole journey. This is called 'orbiting the Earth'. While it is orbiting the Earth it rotates once on its own axis. This is why, as it is moving around the Earth in a circle, the same half of the Moon faces the Earth at all times (Diagram A).

As the Moon orbits the Earth, sometimes it is between the Sun and the Earth and at other times it is further away from the Sun than the Earth is (Diagram A).

When the Moon is directly between the Sun and the Earth, although it is still there, it cannot be seen at night because we cannot see any of the side that is lit up. When this happens we call it the 'new moon'. The sky is black and the Moon is invisible (Diagram A).

When the Moon is on the other side of the Earth, in line with the Sun, then we are able to see all of the side facing the Earth. It looks like a great big white shining disc because light is reflecting from the whole of the Moon's surface which is facing the Earth. This is called a 'full moon'. The other side of the Moon is of course in darkness (Diagram B).

It takes around 14 days to move from full moon to new moon. During this journey, the same part of the Moon is facing the Earth, but less and less of this side of the Moon is being lit by the Sun. As a result, the Moon appears to get smaller each night and changes its shape until it disappears altogether when it reaches the new moon position.

Of course, the same thing happens during the next 14 days except that the Moon appears to grow as it moves back towards the full moon position.

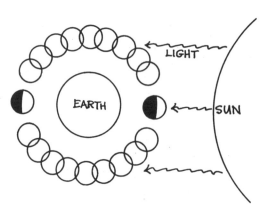

Diagram B

The Moon is always there, a rotating ball of rock. It never changes. It is the light and the movement that make it seem to change.

Sheet C

Note from the Ministry of Exploration

Dear children,

Your assistance is required in helping a small family we have discovered in the mountains of a volcanic island in the Pacific Ocean which is about to blow up. We think they are descendants of people shipwrecked three hundred years ago and they have never left their mountain home. We are giving them a new home in your neighbourhood. The children will be coming to your school. At the moment they believe the Moon does not exist during the day. Here are a tape recording and transcript of their own explanation for the way night and day occur.

> In the beginning the family of white lights twinkling in the great black sky were happy and contented. But after a while they said, "We shall have something to amuse ourselves. Let us make a son and a daughter to give us pleasure. We will each give them some of our own light so that they will be brighter than any one of us and we will all be able to watch them play.
>
> And so they made themselves a son. A great yellow ball, fierce and brave but not very smart. Then they made themselves a daughter. A shimmering white ball, smaller than the son but clever and spiteful.
>
> At first there was great happiness in the great black sky and the family of white lights enjoyed watching their new son and daughter playing together.
>
> But before long their children began to argue and fight. There were great quarrels. The daughter was jealous of the shining yellow robes of her larger brother. She would play cruel tricks on him, leaving him fierce with anger. He, in turn, would reply with great violence, leaving dark bruises all over her glowing white body.
>
> In the end the twinkling lights of the great black sky decided the children must play alone. The son would play in the day and the daughter at night.

Their parents are keen that their children are fully up to date with scientific knowledge, so they can be as happy as possible with us.

Please explain to them <u>clearly</u> why there is a day and a night and why the Moon seems to disappear in the day and is seen clearly at night.

Yours sincerely

R Clearworthy

Commander Rufus Clearworthy, OBE, VC, DFC

Sheet D

Writing
across the
Curriculum

Speaking and listening planning sheet

Names of children in group	Roles
Purpose of oral presentation/objectives	What do we know about audience (for example prior knowledge)

Brainstorm of ideas	
Essential information we must include	Visual aids/drama we could use

Sequence	**Notes**	**Visual aids/Drama**
Introduction	* *	
Point 1	* *	
Point 2	* *	
Point 3	* *	
Close (ending)	* *	
Evaluation		

Sheet E

How day and night occur

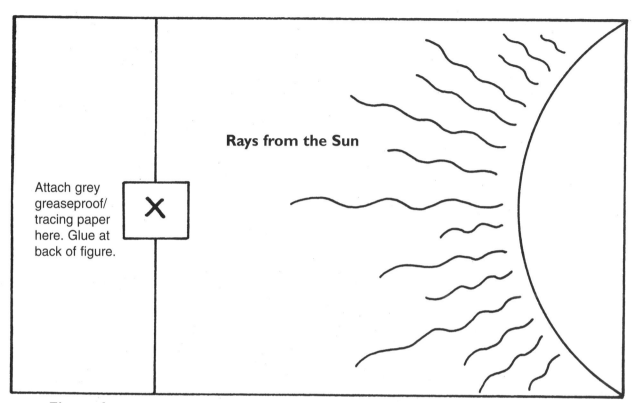

Rays from the Sun

Attach grey greaseproof/tracing paper here. Glue at back of figure.

X

Figure 1

Figure 2:
The Earth

Instructions

You need
Scissors
Split pin
Colouring crayons
Grey greaseproof/tracing paper

What to do
1. Cut out the picture of the Earth (Figure 2) and colour it in. Great Britain is on the edge where the figure of a child is.
2. Colour in the Sun on Figure 1.
3. Use the split pin to attach the Earth to Figure 1 where X is.
4. Stick greaseproof/tracing paper over area indicated, gluing behind the figure so that the Earth can spin freely.

Chapter 5

Persuasion writing

What is a persuasion text?

A persuasion text argues the case for a belief or issue from a particular point of view. The point of view is supported by evidence and reasoning.

Examples of persuasive texts include: advertisements, travel brochures, letters to express a point of view.

Structural features

- Usually begins with an opening statement to indicate the point of view to be expressed

- Main body of text lists the arguments for the point of view supported by evidence and reasoning

- Ends with a conclusion that reiterates the opening statement and presents a summary of the arguments presented.

Linguistic features

- Present tense

- General terms usually used (such as 'people should' rather than 'Mr Jones should')

- Use of connectives to show logic (therefore, however, because of, due to, despite, this shows, in spite of, as a result of)

- Often uses rhetorical questions addressed directly to the reader (Can you believe?)

- Alliterative sentences (in advertisements especially)

- Emotive and persuasive language

- Use of pictures/illustrations to gain an emotional response from the reader

Teaching persuasion writing

It is incredibly easy for children to express their opinions but giving reasons for these opinions is not so simple! Children need lots of oral practice in determining the reasons behind their opinions before they can begin to write them.

When writing persuasively children need to know their subject well and be able to provide supporting evidence (facts or believable fiction) as well as predicting any possible counter arguments. It is vital that they have lots of opportunities to read examples of persuasion writing in order to be able to identify the features and evaluate the success of different persuasive devices before actually trying them out themselves.

The purpose of the text is of the utmost importance. What does the writer want the reader to do in response? Having a clear idea of the proposed outcome will ensure the children experience more successful planning and completion of the writing.

Persuasion writing – progression

Persuasion texts are introduced in Year 3 through letter writing (Term 3: T16).

In Year 4 children read, compare and evaluate examples of arguments, look at how arguments are presented and how statistics and graphs can be used to support arguments and investigate how style and vocabulary are used to convince the reader (Term 3: T16, T17, T18). They assemble and sequence points in order to plan the presentation of a point of view, using writing frames to back up points of view with illustrations and examples and to present the point of view in the form of a letter, script or report (Term 3: T21, T22, T23). They evaluate adverts for their impact, appeal and honesty and design their own (Term 3: T19, T25).

In **Year 5** children read and evaluate letters intended to persuade. They collect and investigate persuasive devices. They write group letters for real issues, write commentaries on an issue and construct and present an argument to the class (Term 3: T12, T14, T15, T17, T18, T19).

In Year 6 the focus moves on to recognising how effective arguments are constructed and actually constructing one, themselves (Term 2: T15, T16, T18).

Unit 1

Lesson focus

History Unit 11 – What was it like for poor children living in Victorian Britain?

Overall aim

To write a persuasive letter presenting a point of view about Victorian child labour.

History emphasis

In this unit the children are required to find out about the lives of poor Victorian children, how attitudes towards them changed and about the people who helped to bring about these changes. They are expected to collect information from a variety of sources and are asked to make conclusions about the Victorian period, presenting their findings in a variety of ways to demonstrate their understanding.

Literacy links

Year 5, Term 3: T12, T13, T14, T15, T17, T19

About this unit

To carry out the work in this unit, the children need to have a reasonable concept of the working conditions of poor Victorian children. They may have read extracts from Charles Dickens' novels or *The Water Babies* by Charles Kingsley and looked at information about the number of working children and the jobs they did. They should also know about people who helped working children (Lord Shaftesbury and Dr Barnardo, for example) and understand that laws and acts of parliament were passed at this time. In literacy, they should have done some work on persuasion writing and understand that its purpose is to convince the reader of a point of view. The unit can be taught over a period of a week during literacy and/or history time.

Switching on

Learning objectives

■ To learn more about the lives of poor children in Victorian times.

■ To recognise and identify the features of persuasion writing.

Resources

■ Sheets A and B (pages 104 and 105)

What to do

Ask the children to tell you what they have already learned about the lives of poor children in Victorian times. What jobs did those children do? Can they explain why some Victorian children worked?

Enlarge Sheet B and display the top half, which is an article that appeared in a Victorian newspaper. Read the article with the children. Ask them what the article is about (the benefits of child labour). Ask the children to

identify the facts. Can we tell what the writer thinks? Why/why not? Explain to the children that news articles often contain 'bias' and that this is when the writer writes things from one point of view; they don't openly give their personal opinions but the reader can tell whether the writer is for or against the thing that he/she is writing about. What sentences or words in the article might give us clues about what the writer thinks? What do children think about the article? Do they agree or disagree with the points the article makes? It is important to remember that there are no right or wrong answers when discussing opinions. However, they should be able to give reasons for their answers and justify their opinions.

Ask the children what they know about persuasive writing. Do they know what the purpose is? Can they give any examples of when it might be used? Display an enlarged version of the top part of Sheet A and discuss the meaning of each feature mentioned (or use Sheet A as your guide to point out each feature on Sheet B).

Now read the letter extract at the bottom of Sheet B together, explaining that a newspaper reader wrote this letter in response to the article they have just read. What is the person's opinion? Why is it easier to know the writer's opinion in the letter than it was in the article? Use Sheet A to help.

Ask the children to work in pairs to highlight any persuasive words or sentences. Discuss their responses, making sure that they are able to explain why it is persuasive. How effective do they think the letter is? Can they think of any ways that the letter could be made more effective? Refer to Sheet A to see if the letter fulfils all the criteria.

Plenary

Ask the children to tell you the features of a persuasive text. Make a checklist of their suggestions that can be referred to later on (include all those listed on page 98 of this book).

NB: The next two sessions, 'Revving up' and 'Taking off', can be taught as two separate sessions or one after the other as an extended lesson of approximately two hours.

Revving up

Learning objectives

■ To be able to suggest reasons for Victorian points of view.

■ To develop persuasion writing skills using reasoning and evidence.

Resource

■ Sheet C (page 106)

What to do

Start the lesson by making an outrageous statement, such as 'All children are lazy,' or '... football team is rubbish.' It is likely that this will spark a response in the children who will probably give an immediate opinion of their outrage. If not, invite them to tell you what they think of your statement. Can they think of any ways that you could convince them to agree with you? Ask them what you would need to do to persuade them. You should be able to elicit the need for 'proof' or evidence to support your opinion. Remind them about yesterday's discussion and how you explained that there was no right or wrong answer unless you can support them with evidence. You should give reasons for your opinions.

Provide the children with a copy of the list of Victorian opinions about child labour (Sheet C). Read through the opinions. Ask the children to work in pairs to sort the opinions into two columns, one for and one against child labour – they could cut them out to sort them.

Explain that all the statements are real opinions of different people in Victorian times but on their own they do nothing to persuade or influence the reader. Ask the children to work through the opinions and try to think of a reason to support them. They could also make a suggestion about who might have had such an opinion.

Discuss the children's responses and suggested reasons. What did they find easy/hard? Why? (They are likely to tell you that it is hard to think of reasons to support opinions that you don't agree with yourself.)

Return to your outrageous statement. Tell the children that although you know they do not agree, you are going to try and support your opinion with some reasons and evidence. Model writing persuasively (use the text below to help you), talking to the children about what you are thinking as you write, and refer to the checklist collated in the 'Switching on' session. Tell them that they should just watch and listen at first and that they should consider your arguments before they express their opinions.

Following is a script **for your eyes only** which you can use or adapt. The text in italics is what you say out loud as if to yourself, the text in bold is what you write.

Okay, I want to try and convince you that I was right when I said 'All children are lazy.'

I want to start by making an opening statement that lets the reader know what I am writing about. **Research shows** – *this makes it sound like it is a proven fact* – **that today's children are far less active than children in the past.** *Good, I just need to check that I'm writing in the present tense. Yes, I've used 'are' so that's right. I now need to give an example of a problem.* **Because of this** *(connective of logic to show cause and effect)***, children are at increased risk of heart disease and obesity.**

Right, (reread opening) *I now want to write my arguments to support my statement and I need to think about what other people might say so that I can use that to help me convince people who might disagree. New paragraph…* **Children today lead very inactive lives due to** *(connective of logic again)* **the increasing popularity of videos, DVDs and computer games. Many children** *(I'm making a general statement about children, not anyone in particular)* **spend hours in front of a television or computer screen, which means that they are not physically active for long periods at a time.** *I haven't said anything about what people who disagree might say so I need to do that now…* **While some people may argue that this helps to improve children's knowledge and creativity, surely no one can deny that children need physical exercise and**

fresh air to keep them healthy. *I'm pleased with that bit because I've directed it at the reader to make them think.*

Okay, new paragraph. I need to support my claims some more… **As well as the lack of exercise, it can also be argued** *(shows that it is an opinion, not a fact)* **that children are becoming less independent. They have little need to think for themselves when everything is ready in an instant. Action movies have taken over from adventure stories and fewer children are reading for pleasure because they prefer to sit in front of a video or DVD.** *I could continue to give more arguments to support my opinion but I don't want to take up all your time so I am now going to move on to my conclusion. I need to repeat my point of view and try and make one last persuasive comment to the reader.*

New paragraph. **There is no doubt that children are less active and that many prefer to play computer games instead of sport. Any intelligent person** *(obviously the reader will think that he or she is one)* **must be able to see that this is a sure sign of children's lazy attitudes to work and life in general.**

Read through and alter any bits you wish to change. Pick out the features and explain that, while you understand that you won't have convinced them (because it is an outrageous statement), you have made them think about the issue and begin to see that there are reasons to support your opinion.

When you have finished ask the children if your opinion seems more reasonable now. Tell them that they don't have to agree with you, but they need to think about whether it is still outrageous or if it makes sense.

Plenary

Ask the children to work in pairs to come up with some statements of their own, such as 'All adults are fit and healthy' and, working together, suggest two or three opinions that are supported by 'evidence'. They could then share their ideas with another pair and try and convince them of their opinions. Share the children's ideas. How easy was it to convince others of their arguments?

Taking off

Learning objectives

- ■ To be able to support opinions with reason.
- ■ To develop persuasive skills orally as part of a debate.
- ■ To develop understanding of Victorian views about child labour.

Resource

- ■ Sheet D (page 107)

What to do

Make copies of Sheet D and read it through with the whole class. Then split the class into two groups. Cut the sheet in two and give one set of views to each group. Tell the children that they are going to hold a debate; the group that represents the employers will advocate child labour and the group that represents the reformists will oppose it. Explain that it doesn't matter if they don't actually agree with the point they are arguing as they need to put themselves in the role of someone who does think that. Remind them that in order to be truly persuasive they need not only to think about reasons for their point of view but also to consider the views of their opponents and predict what they might say in support of their points. When they have made this prediction they can then use it to their advantage by dismissing or answering opposing concerns.

Give the children time to discuss their views in their group. Each group (or you) might want to appoint one or two scribes to record their ideas in note form so that they can refer to them during the debate.

Set out your rules for holding the debate; make it clear that only one person may speak at a time and that each side will be given a chance to respond to comments made by the other, everyone in the group should make at least one point and points should be supported. Tell the children that there will be a reward for the most persuasive group (depending on what your school reward system is) and that you will listen carefully to all points made.

Allow time for the debate. You may want to hold this in a separate lesson, perhaps after lunch or by using a history lesson.

Plenary

Briefly recap the main points made by each side. Explain which views you think were the most persuasive and say why. A tick sheet or score sheet could be used to 'mark' each group. For example, award marks out of ten for working together, listening, speaking and supporting arguments with reasons. Write this up on a flip chart and ask the children to evaluate their own performance and that of the 'other side'. Discuss their feelings about the debate. What did they find easy/hard? What would they change/ do differently?

Flying solo

Learning objective

■ To write a persuasive letter.

Resources

■ Sheets B and E (pages 105 and 108)
■ Checklist of the features of persuasion writing

What to do

By now the children should have lots of ideas and reasons for supporting the use of child labour or for abolishing it. Tell them that it is now up to them to make up their own minds and decide what they think, based on everything they have learned.

Reread the article (Sheet B). Remind the children of the letter that was written in response to this being published in a Victorian newspaper. Explain that they will be writing their own letter, trying to persuade readers of their point of view. Go over the structure and features of persuasion writing to recap.

Model writing the opening paragraph of a letter. There are two examples given below, one for each point of view. These are intended for you to use when modelling the writing for the children; they should not see them. The bold text is what you write and the italics are what to say out loud as if to yourself. Remember that you are only demonstrating the opening paragraph.

I am going to write a letter in response to the newspaper article that we looked at earlier in the week. We have looked at lots of arguments for and against child labour in Victorian times and I hope that you can now make up your own minds and decide what you think for yourselves. You are then going to write your own persuasive letter to convince the readers that you are right.

I am going to show you how to begin your letter and we are going to use the checklist of features to help us.

*I'm going to use the same opening as the first letter because I think it starts well…. **I am writing to you in response to an article featured in your publication last week.***

I now need to state my point of view and I want to present it as a fact before going on to my main paragraphs giving evidence and reasons to support my opinions…

Children are a valuable resource in our growing industries. They provide affordable labour and are an effective workforce, helping to improve the wealth of our country.

or…

Children are being crippled and even killed because of poor working conditions. Children as young as four are being forced to work in unhealthy and dangerous conditions for very little money.

I can now go on to state my arguments and support them with evidence. I need to make sure that I use persuasive language and draw my points together with a conclusion at the end.

Ask the children to draft their letter, using Sheet E to help them if they want. You can work with individuals or a small group depending on the needs of the class. It is a good idea to provide them with a bank of useful phrases.

Give the children time to proofread or peer mark their letters. Best copies may be produced for homework.

Plenary

Choose one or two examples to be evaluated as a class by asking for volunteers to provide their work. Together, identify the good parts and make suggestions for improvement. Ask the children what they have learned during this unit.

Writing
across the
Curriculum

opening
statement to
say what the
article is about

connective

Children at work

Families living in city slums have discovered a new way to increase their weekly income.

facts

By sending children out to work, families can receive additional wages and therefore make paying the rent and bills easier and more manageable. Children as young as four are being sent to work in factories and mills. The long hours worked by the children provide the families with minimal wages that can be used to supplement the parents' income.

could
indicate an
opinion

could
indicate
opinion

Owners of factories and mills are encouraging the use of children as workers because they can pay them lower wages than adults, thus keeping their outgoings to a minimum whilst maximising profits. As well as taking low wages, the children are easier to control and less likely to complain about poor working conditions. It seems that factory owners and families are on to a winner: using children as workers helps bosses line their pockets and parents pay the rent.

present
tense

Noone knows the effects of this type of labour on young bodies but the trend looks set to continue as more factories and mills are built and more and more families move out of the countryside and into towns in search of work.

conclusion

opening
statement
gives reason
for writing

Extract taken from a letter written to the newspaper

I am writing to you in response to an article featured in your publication last week.

I was appalled to discover that children as young as four are being sent to work in mills and factories. Surely this is barbaric and cruel? How can children be expected to work shifts of 16 hours?

addresses
reader
directly –
rhetorical
question

use
of personal
pronoun to
show opinion

Whilst I accept that poor families are in desperate need of extra income, I feel that I must point out the dangers of using children as cheap labour. Many of these children are already malnourished and in poor health; being forced to work in cramped, stuffy, noisy conditions can cause crippling diseases. On top of this, children are treated like slaves and whipped and punished for talking or working too slowly.

If children are forced to work in such conditions then I feel certain that many of them will not grow up to become adults. The only people benefiting from child labour are the owners of factories and mills who are just lining their pockets.

statement
of opinion
presented as fact

conclusion

Children at work

Families living in city slums have discovered a new way to increase their weekly income.

By sending children out to work, families can receive additional wages and therefore make paying the rent and bills easier and more manageable. Children as young as four are being sent to work in factories and mills. The long hours worked by the children provide the families with minimal wages that can be used to supplement the parents' income.

Owners of factories and mills are encouraging the use of children as workers because they can pay them lower wages than adults, thus keeping their outgoings to a minimum whilst maximising profits. As well as taking low wages, the children are easier to control and less likely to complain about poor working conditions. It seems that factory owners and families are on to a winner: using children as workers helps bosses line their pockets and parents pay the rent.

Noone knows the effects of this type of labour on young bodies but the trend looks set to continue as more factories and mills are built and more and more families move out of the countryside and into towns in search of work.

Extract taken from a letter written to the newspaper

I am writing to you in response to an article featured in your publication last week.

I was appalled to discover that children as young as four are being sent to work in mills and factories. Surely this is barbaric and cruel? How can children be expected to work shifts of 16 hours?

Whilst I accept that poor families are in desperate need of extra income, I feel that I must point out the dangers of using children as cheap labour. Many of these children are already malnourished and in poor health; being forced to work in cramped, stuffy, noisy conditions can cause crippling diseases. On top of this, children are treated like slaves and whipped and punished for talking or working too slowly.

If children are forced to work in such conditions then I feel certain that many of them will not grow up to become adults. The only people benefiting from child labour are the owners of factories and mills who are just lining their pockets.

Victorian views

"Children who end up living on the streets are too lazy or stupid to work."

"Many children become sick and deformed from working long hours in such poor conditions."

"It is the duty of the middle and upper classes to help these poor, destitute children."

"We need children to work in the mills because they cost less than adults."

"I need a climbing boy to sweep my chimney properly."

"The use of young boys to clean chimneys is barbaric and unnecessary."

"It is cruel to make children work such long hours for such little money."

"There are too many homeless children. We cannot support them all so they should work to support themselves."

"Children should be educated so that they can get a better job in the future."

Victorian points of view

Employers

- There are not enough workers in the mills, factories and mines. In order to make enough products or mine enough coal we need to supplement the workforce with child labour.

- Children cost less than adults so we can give more people jobs so there are less unemployed.

- Children are able to do some jobs that adults can't because of their size (adults can't squeeze into small spaces under machines or up chimneys).

- If the children didn't work they would just end up living on the street or in the workhouse.

- Children are paid fair wages, they do not have to pay any bills and their wages increase as they get older.

- If children work it benefits the family by generating an extra income.

Reformists

- Children are often injured or killed at work because they are not supervised and machinery is not made safe.

- Diseases are easily spread or caused in the poor conditions; chimney sweeps are likely to get lung disease and children working in match factories can be poisoned by the phosphorus.

- Children are beaten and treated like slaves.

- After long periods of heavy labour children become crippled because their bodies are not given the chance to grow properly and naturally if they are twisted into confined spaces or carrying heavy loads.

- Children should be educated to read and write so that they can get a good job when they are older.

- The working day is much too long.

Sheet E

Opening
(Say why you are writing and make a statement that expresses your point of view.)

Arguments
(Support your opinions with reasons and evidence. Ask your reader rhetorical questions.)

Conclusion
(Summarise your arguments and end with a persuasive comment directed at the reader.)

Unit 2

Lesson focus

Citizenship Unit 7 – Children's rights – human rights

Overall aim

To produce a persuasive leaflet or poster advocating children's rights, with reference to the United Nations Conventions for the Rights of the Child.

Citizenship emphasis

In this unit the children explore the different types of rights and responsibilities they have/will have during their lives. It helps to develop a sense of responsibility and understanding about their roles as citizens. Children also look at the different groups and organisations that campaign for children's rights and welfare in order to increase their awareness.

Literacy links

Year 5, Term 3: T13, T14, T15, T19

About this unit

The children should be familiar with the features of persuasive writing (see the beginning of this chapter) and have had experience of a range of persuasive texts.

These sessions would be best taught during PSHE and citizenship and should follow an initial discussion or brainstorming session about rights and responsibilities children have. This unit focuses on group work and cooperation and the children should be given opportunities to work together. There are several organisations who provide information and resources and it may be worth contacting them prior to this unit. Within this unit, the articles from the convention are reproduced with the kind permission of Save the Children. You can also look out for publications such as *Stand Up, Speak Out*, a book about children's rights (Two-Can Publishing, 2001).

Switching on

Learning objective

■ To become familiar with the articles (rights) of the UN Convention for the Rights of the Child.

Resources

■ Sheet A (page 112)

What to do

Before the lesson, plan groups for the children to work in. Photocopy and cut up enough copies of Sheet A so that there is one cut up version per group (you may want to enlarge it to A3). It is important to be aware that different children will have had different experiences, when considering these rights, so children's opinions need to be handled with care and sensitivity.

Tell the children that they will be looking at children's rights. Explain that the United Nations produced a document that officially states the rights of children. Tell them that it has been signed by the leaders of the world,

apart from the USA and Somalia (children may want to discuss this further – that is entirely up to you but a homework challenge might be useful). Briefly discuss (and list on a flip chart or board) what rights the children would expect to see in the convention. Tell them that there are 54 articles (or rights) altogether, and that articles 43–54 are about what governments will do. The first article identifies a child as anyone under 18 and says that all the rights apply to all children.

Give out the cut up version of Sheet A, which contains simplified versions of some of the articles (rights) and tell the children that they are to work in groups to look at the children's rights stated in the convention. They have to sort the rights and decide which they think are the most/least important. They should be prepared to discuss and give reasons for their opinions. (This activity provides excellent opportunities for speaking and listening and it will be interesting to spend some time with each group.)

Read through the articles with the children and explain anything they are unsure of. Give them 20 to 30 minutes (as necessary) to rank them. Appoint a spokesperson for each group.

Plenary

Ask the spokesperson to give their top three rights and explain the group's reasoning. (Make sure you give the spokespeople time to think, plan and talk with the rest of the group. If there is time, you may wish to also share the last right on their list.)

Revving up

Learning objectives

- To be able to express opinions and provide reasons to support the importance of/need for children's rights.
- To identify emotive devices used in persuasion.
- To write emotive arguments.

Resources

- Sheet A (page 112), already cut up from 'Switching on'
- Sheets B and C (pages 113 and 114)

What to do

Remind the children of the work done in the last session. Display an enlarged version of Sheet C or give the children their own copies. Explain that when writers are trying to be persuasive they often use people's emotions (anger, sympathy, guilt, sadness and joy) to help get their point across. We have all seen the sad images in the RSPCA and NSPCC adverts and the shocking pictures in the anti-smoking and drink-driving campaigns. Pictures can be very powerful but words can also be emotive.

Read through the sheet. Explain that it is attempting to persuade people of the importance of one of the articles (rights). Can they suggest which one it is referring to?

Ask the children to highlight any words or phrases that they think have an emotional effect on the reader. Add their ideas to the enlarged version of the text. Draw their attention to any other special features of persuasive writing in the text (refer to Sheet B). Make a checklist of these.

Now ask them to work in pairs to write emotive arguments for one or two of the rights from Sheet A.

Plenary

Ask the pairs to feed back their arguments. Can the rest of the class identify the relevant right/article? Do the arguments generate an emotional response?

Taking off

Learning objectives

- To generate arguments advocating children's rights.
- To use emotive devices for persuasion.
- To plan a persuasive poster.

Resources

- Sheets A, D and E (pages 112, 115 and 116)
- The children's work from the last session
- Checklist of features from 'Revving up'

What to do

Explain to the children that they have been developing their skills of persuasion and have been working very hard (possibly without even knowing it). Tell them that over the next two sessions they will be producing a poster to persuade people of the importance of children's rights. Remind them that they have been looking at emotive devices and that they will need to use these in their posters, which will be informative and persuasive.

Share an enlarged version of Sheet E. Ask the children to identify the emotive devices (use Sheet D as your guide) and any other persuasive techniques.

Tell the children to choose one, two or three articles/ rights (the quantity given can be used as differentiation) from Sheet A. They need to come up with persuasive arguments for each one and then think about how they could present these on a poster and perhaps add pictures, using Sheet E as a model.

Ask them to make a plan of their poster.

Plenary

Ask them to swap plans with a partner. Display the features checklist and ask the partners to tick each feature found. Do they need to add/amend their plans in the light of this?

Flying solo

Learning objective

■ To produce a persuasive poster advocating children's rights.

Resources

■ Poster plans from the last session
■ Colouring pens/pencils
■ A3 paper
■ Checklist of features

What to do

Explain to the children that they will be producing their posters in this session. Remind them of the checklist and tell them that the posters will go on display in the school. (If possible it would be good to display the posters and the articles and any other resources you may have, somewhere prominent such as an entrance or school hall.)

Give them time to produce their posters, supporting them where necessary.

Plenary

Ask each child (in turn) to come to the front of the class with their poster. Ask them to say two things they are pleased with/that they think they have done well and identify areas for improvement. Other class members may also be encouraged to give positive feedback.

Children's rights

According to the United Nations Convention, all children have the right to:

2. not be discriminated against	22. special protection if they are a refugee
3. have their best interests considered when adults make decisions about them	23. special care and education to help them develop and lead a full life if they have a disability
4. have their rights ensured by the government	24. get the best health care possible
5. be helped and guided by parents and family	25. be looked after and receive regular visits if they are looked after away from home
6. life	26. help from the government if they are poor or in need
7. a name and nationality	27. a good standard of living to help them develop properly
8. an identity	28. education
9. live with their parents unless this is bad for them	29. education that tries to develop their personality, skills and interests as much as possible, while teaching values and respect
10. leave any country and go to live in their own country with their parents	30. speak their own language, worship their own religion and celebrate their culture
11. be protected from being kidnapped	31. play and free time
12. say what they think and be listened to by adults	32. be protected from work that is bad for their health
13. get information and express an opinion	33. be protected from exposure to taking, selling and making dangerous drugs
14. think what they like and choose their religion (with their parents' guidance)	34. be protected from any form of abuse
15. meet other children and join clubs or groups	35. not be abducted or sold
16. privacy	36. be protected from exploitation
17. have access to information that is relevant: for example, television, video, radio, newspapers and magazines	37. not be punished cruelly and not be put in prison with adults
18. be brought up by their parents if possible	38. not be allowed in an army or fight in a war if they are under 15
19. be protected from violence, neglect and abuse	39. help if they have been hurt, neglected or badly treated
20. special care and protection if they can't live with their parents	40. help in defending themselves and have their age taken into account if they break the law
21. get the best care available if they are adopted	41. share the same rights and laws of their country if they give them better rights than these
	42. have everyone know about the rights in the convention: the government should tell people

Sheet B

The rights of the child

opening
statement

emotive
word/
phrase

present
tense

connective

Most children in our country are lucky enough to have a
comfortable home, plenty of food, clothing and a family who love
them. Unfortunately, there are still some children who live their
lives in poverty – these children do not have a standard of living
that is good enough to help them develop.

In order to grow into healthy, confident adults, children need to
get a good start in life. Imagine what it would be like to have no
house, barely enough food and no safe water to drink. Some
children have to battle with these problems every day: they have
nowhere they can feel safe, they are malnourished and they will
not grow or develop properly. They are exposed to disease and
illness every time they drink or have a wash – it's a miracle they
reach adulthood at all.

emotive
word/
phrase

persuasive
language

Surely everyone knows that this is a terrible way to live? Don't
children have rights too? Isn't it our responsibility to protect and
look after them? Only cruel and ignorant people would be able to
turn a blind eye. We have signed the UN Convention for the
Rights of the Child. We live in a civilised, developed country, don't
we? If so, then we must do something to make sure that the rights
of children are valued and protected. Everyone, no matter what
age they are, has the right to a good standard of living.

rhetorical
question

arguments
for the point of
view are listed,
supported by
reasons

concluding
statement

general
terms used,
such as
'everyone' and
'people'

The rights of the child

Most children in our country are lucky enough to have a comfortable home, plenty of food, clothing and a family who love them. Unfortunately, there are still some children who live their lives in poverty – these children do not have a standard of living that is good enough to help them develop.

In order to grow into healthy, confident adults, children need to get a good start in life. Imagine what it would be like to have no house, barely enough food and no safe water to drink. Some children have to battle with these problems every day: they have nowhere they can feel safe, they are malnourished and they will not grow or develop properly. They are exposed to disease and illness every time they drink or have a wash – it's a miracle they reach adulthood at all.

Surely everyone knows that this is a terrible way to live? Don't children have rights too? Isn't it our responsibility to protect and look after them? Only cruel and ignorant people would be able to turn a blind eye. We have signed the UN Convention for the Rights of the Child. We live in a civilised, developed country, don't we? If so, then we must do something to make sure that the rights of children are valued and protected. Everyone, no matter what age they are, has the right to a good standard of living.

LOOK AFTER OUR CHILDREN

Every child has the right to:

EDUCATION!

'Peter' cannot read or write. When he is older he will only be able to do hard, manual labour for very low wages. He has no hope of getting a good job without a good education.

Do you want to be responsible for the death of a child? Children need an education so that they can learn to make the right choices in their life.

CRC Article 28

- the emphasis on 'every' signals all children are equal
- emotive language
- powerful images to give idea of what might happen
- no education = worst case scenario (shock?)
- strong, final and emotive, implies it is too late (no second chances)
- gives reason why education is so important
- uses facts to inform reader of Peter's problems and perhaps provoke sympathy, anger, action
- directed at reader, makes it personal
- picture to pull at heart-strings (sympathy)
- reference to the convention article

Every child has the right to:

'Peter' cannot read or write. When he is older he will only be able to do hard, manual labour for very low wages. He has no hope of getting a good job without a good education.

EDUCATION!

Do you want to be responsible for the death of a child? Children need an education so that they can learn to make the right choices in their life.

CRC Article 28

Chapter 6

Note making

What is note making?

Firstly, it is important to distinguish between note making and note taking. Notes are 'made' from secondary sources such as books, videos and so on, whereas notes are 'taken' from first hand, primary sources such as observations and discussions.

Note making is a form of information retrieval. In order to find anything out for ourselves we need to: do it, see it, experience it, hear it or read about it. Note making happens when children use work produced by someone else (such as books) to help them organise and develop their own ideas using information available. Notes act as a 'memory jogger' or 'idea prompt' and are used to make a record of important (or 'key') pieces of information that can then be used to create a new, original piece of writing. Note making is not about copying chunks of someone else's work; it is about picking out relevant bits of information that refer to a specific task or topic.

The purpose of making notes is to communicate information in an informal way; it is about manipulating and interpreting ideas and is a way of remembering.

Note making techniques

- Grids/tables – used to compare information on a similar theme; useful for non-chronological writing
- Marking texts – highlighting, underlining, crossing out – a form of selection and rejection
- Summarising – condensing relevant information
- Patterning – underlining then listing key words before grouping
- Pictures/symbols – using pictures or symbols to represent ideas – useful for instructions and explanations as well as assessing children's understanding

Teaching note making

There is no 'one way' of making notes – they only have to be meaningful to the person using them. However, in order to make effective/useful notes, children need to be taught the skills of note making.

The whole point of making notes is to develop understanding and reading for meaning, so it is important to have a clear purpose – encourage children to ask 'Why?' when making notes. Without a clear purpose, finding 'key' words/phrases can be meaningless because 'key information' could be different for every child, depending on their experience and interests. This is why it is useful to use questions that guide the note making.

When writing notes up into connected prose it is important to allow a period of time (at least a few hours) after making the notes. This allows the child to remember the information, using their notes, and to move away from the original text and structure – eliminating the problem of copying from the original source.

Note making – progression

Children are introduced to note making in KS1 where they are taught to locate information, find key words and phrases and produce simple flow charts and diagrams (Year 1, Term 2: T25; Year 2, Term 2: T21; Term 3: T19).

In Year 3 children continue to develop their skills of locating information and recording what they have found out (Term 1: T18, T21; Term 2: T17, Term 3: T17, T19, T25).

In Year 4 children develop skills of skimming and scanning to locate information and are encouraged to record the information gathered from several sources in one simple format. They are expected to be able to summarise in writing the key ideas from a source (Term 2: T15, T16, T17, T18, T20, T21, T22, T23; Term 3: T20, T24).

In **Year 5** the children are encouraged to discuss the purpose of note making and how this influences the type of notes they make. They are expected to locate information confidently and efficiently and make notes for different purposes, using abbreviations where appropriate. They decide when to use their own words and when to copy, quote and adapt (Term 1: T23, T26, T27; Term 2: T17, T20, T21; Term 3: T16). These skills are consolidated in Year 6 (Term 3: T18).

Unit 1

Lesson focus

History Unit 14 – Who were the Ancient Greeks?

Overall aim

To produce a set of notes comparing Greek gods and to use these notes to write an original information text.

History emphasis

In this unit, children are encouraged to find out about Ancient Greek life and customs, myths, legends and beliefs. The children should have some understanding of Greek life and customs and be aware of the significance of Mount Olympus and the Greek underworld. They should have heard, or read, some of the stories about the Greek gods which contain useful information about their powers and attributes.

Literacy links

Year 5, Term 2: T16, T17, T21, T29

About this unit

The following lessons can form part of history lessons or the literacy hour. They could be taught as a continuous lesson but there should be a space of time between 'Taking off' and 'Flying solo' in order to allow the children to work from their own notes without referring to the original text.

The children should have had experience of reading information texts and understanding the conventions of reading non-narrative texts.

Throughout this unit the children will use charts to collect information in note form. This method of note making helps them to make comparisons, as they can record information under the same headings. You may wish to limit the children to researching only a few gods or allocate certain gods to specific groups in order to develop a biographical class dictionary of gods. The texts will work best if they are supplemented with extracts from other reference books so that the children can experience making notes from a range of texts.

Switching on

Learning objectives

■ To evaluate a range of information books.
■ To develop an understanding of the need for relevant questions in note making.

Resources

■ Information books about Ancient Greece – enough for one between two
■ Scrap paper

What to do

Explain to the children that over the next few sessions they will be finding out about some of the Greek gods and making notes so that they can eventually write their own information texts for other children (you can specify a year group).

Ask them what they think note making is/involves. Tell them that before they can make notes they need to be able to identify what it is they want to find out and that they can do this by asking questions. It is important to explain that, sometimes, published books might not be useful – if they cannot find the information they want, it is just as likely to be due to a text that is too difficult, not relevant, badly laid out and so on (rather than being a problem with them!). It is empowering for children to question things: just because a book is published doesn't mean it is going to be useful.

Give out the information books, one between two. Tell the children that they are not allowed to open the book or look inside. Explain that they can read and use any information they can find on the front and back covers only. Ask the children (in their pairs) to write down three questions that they think they would be able to answer by looking inside the book. Allow five minutes or so for the children to generate their questions, supporting those who need help. (It may also be useful to prepare questions about a book yourself.)

After five minutes tell the children to swap books, and questions, with another pair. Challenge them to find the answers inside the books – remind them that they must find the answer in the book and not use their existing knowledge, even if they know the answer. This activity is not testing them; it is testing the books (and the questions). Tell them to record the page numbers of any answers and to think about how they found the information (use of contents, index, skimming, scanning, flicking through, looking at diagrams, pictures, captions and so on).

Allow enough time for the children to look for the answers. Bring them together ready for a class discussion of the task. Ask the following questions:

Who found all the answers?

Who found the answers easily?

Who found it difficult?

Who couldn't answer all the questions?

Who thinks it was difficult because of the questions?

Who thinks it was difficult because of the book?

Plenary

Look at the books and questions of two or three groups. Evaluate the books; do they have contents, index, glossary? Are there useful illustrations and layouts or is it dense text? Now look carefully at the questions; are they relevant or too narrow? What do the children think makes a good question?

Finally, discuss the techniques used for finding the information – make a class list for future reference.

Revving up

Learning objectives

■ To learn about Greek gods.

■ To know how to use a chart/table for note making.

■ To recognise relevant questions.

Resources

■ Sheets A, B and C (pages 123 to 127)

What to do

Tell the children that you are going to work together to make some notes about Greek gods and that you are going to show them how to record their notes so that they are useful. In the next session they will make their own notes in the same way; these will finally be used to help them create a piece of writing about the Greek gods. Ask the children what they can remember from the last session (emphasise the need for purpose and use of focused questions).

Explain that you have prepared some questions to help them with their research and that you would like them to have a look at them and let you know if they think any of the questions are not relevant or would not be useful in finding information. Write the following questions on the board or flip chart:

Did the gods like each other?

Why were the gods important?

What powers did the gods have?

Were the goddesses pretty?

Where did the gods live?

Did everyone believe in the gods?

Were the gods related?

How old were the gods?

What did the gods wear?

What animals were associated with the gods?

The children can work individually, in pairs or in groups to eliminate questions. Share their ideas and, as a class, agree which questions to keep and which to discard.

Provide each child with a copy of Sheet A. Read it through together. Ask the children if they think they can answer the questions they have kept from the list. Choose one god or goddess and ask them to find answers to the questions. This can be done orally or on 'show me' boards. Ask them how you could record your answers without lots of writing. You want your notes to be quick so you don't want to write out the question, or spend time writing proper sentences. Listen to their ideas and then introduce the chart on Sheet B by sharing an enlarged version.

Explain that by using a chart/table you can record all the information you need and can compare the gods at the same time because you will be asking the same questions about each god.

Give the children copies of Sheet B. Together, using the god or goddess you focused on in your earlier discussion, complete the information on the enlarged version of the chart. Show them how to jot down ideas in note form (you could use Sheet C to help you).

Give the children time to reread the text and collect some information about one other god or goddess of their choice.

Plenary

To end the session, briefly discuss the children's opinions about this method of recording notes. How does it help them? How useful do they think it might be when they are doing other kinds of research?

Taking off

Learning objectives

■ To become familiar with the names, powers and attributes of Greek gods.

■ To make notes using a chart.

Resources

■ Sheets A and C (pages 123 – 124 and 126 – 127)

■ Selection of information books about Greek gods

■ The charts (Sheet B) started in last session and some spares

What to do

Remind the children of last session's work using the chart. Can they remember why charts are useful? (To record information, answer questions and compare gods.) Tell them that in this session they will be making notes about other gods.

The children can work in pairs or on their own, depending on the dynamics of the class. (Working together slows down the pace of reading and encourages discussion, meaning that there is greater interaction with the text and more opportunities for developing understanding.)

Reread Sheet A and ask the children to add to their notes using relevant information from the sheets. (It might be a nice idea to get a few children to work on OHTs or to photocopy their work onto OHTs later on.)

Give the children time to fill in their charts (Sheet C contains the relevant information). You will need to support less able pupils; more able pupils could use the information books and other sources as well to research other gods or to add to their existing information.

Plenary

Share some examples of the children's notes – ask for volunteers to come out to the front of the class and briefly talk about one god of their choice, using their notes as a prompt. Make sure you give the children a couple of minutes thinking and planning time before their presentations.

After listening, focus on the use of complete sentences when giving the information and encourage them to think about how they will develop their notes into sentences. Revise sentence structure and punctuation in order to prepare them for writing up their notes in the next session.

Flying solo

Learning objective

■ To be able to use a set of notes to write an information text about Greek gods.

Resource

■ The prepared notes

What to do

Tell the children that they will be using only their notes in this session to write information about the Greek gods and goddesses. (As an added incentive you could say this is for display or a class anthology/information book for the school library.) Explain that it is important to use their own words and make sure that they understand what they are writing.

Use the following notes, which are based on those in the charts on Sheet C, to model writing a paragraph. For this type of writing it is best to use subheadings for each god; it doesn't matter what order they are written in as it will make sense in any order.

The children should not see the text but think that you are really making it up as you go along. The idea is that you show them how to write while explaining your thinking at the same time.

The bold print is what you actually write and the italics can be used as a script of what to say out loud as if to yourself.

Right, I'm going to use the notes in our chart to write about Aphrodite. I will need to use full sentences and include as much information as I can. I guess I am writing a sort of fact file. I'm going to use her name as a title.

Aphrodite

Who was she? **Aphrodite was the goddess of love and beauty. She was considered to be the most beautiful of all the goddesses and was given the precious golden apple as proof of this.** *Now I need to give a little bit more information, still on the subject of her beauty.* **Aphrodite was not only beautiful – everyone desired her. This was because** (*connective to show logic*) **of the magic girdle she wore that made people fall in love with her.**

So, she was beautiful but she wasn't happy in love, was she? What about her husband? I need a connective to show the other side – I can't start a sentence with 'but' – new paragraph.

Despite (*connective*) **her beauty, Aphrodite was not happily married. Her husband was the powerful god of fire, Hephaestus, who was lame and badly deformed. He was as ugly as Aphrodite was beautiful and was jealous of all the attention his wife received.** *I now need to mention Ares and Eros.* **Aphrodite actually loved Ares, the god of war, and together they had a son, Eros – god of love.**

I think that's about it but I haven't mentioned the dove; where would that fit? I don't just want to stick it on the end. I think I'll add it after the first sentence. (Saying this helps the children to see that writing isn't perfect the first time, they need to plan and alter as they write.) So (return to first sentence) **Aphrodite was the goddess of love and beauty;** *semicolon as I am going to continue this sentence,* **she was always associated with a white dove because of the bird's pure and graceful beauty.**

Reread and check that you and the children are happy. Talk about the use of connectives and explain that writing takes shape as you write, but that you need to have some idea of where you're going. Tell the children that they will be able to use their notes to help them write their own pieces of information.

Allow the children time to write their paragraphs. You will need to direct your teaching towards one or two groups. As they write, support and guide their ideas, concentrating on the structure and cohesion of sentences. When they have finished, they should swap and read each other's, making suggestions for improvements or adding illustrations if desired.

Plenary

Share some examples of the children's work and review what they have learned about Greek gods and about note making.

Greek Gods and Goddesses

Greek beliefs

The Ancient Greeks worshipped many gods and believed that Mount Olympus, Greece's highest mountain, was the home of the gods and the site of the golden throne of Zeus, ruler of the gods.

Because people believed that everything was influenced by the gods, they created many temples and celebrated festivals to worship them. The Greeks thought that everything outside human control was created by the immortal gods. Each force of nature was represented by one of the gods, who would cause storms, love, death, crops and harvests depending on whether the Greeks had pleased or displeased them.

The Greeks relied on the assistance of the ever watchful gods but sometimes prayers and sacrifices would go unanswered. Because of this the people began to think that the gods were moody and unpredictable. They still believed, though, that Zeus would eventually punish all crimes and reward good deeds.

Zeus and his brothers

Between them, Zeus and his brothers, Poseidon and Hades, controlled Earth. Zeus ruled the heavens and, as god of thunder, his weapon was a thunderbolt. Zeus is said to have visited Earth many times and loved many women. This made his beautiful wife, Hera, so jealous that she hated him. Hera was the goddess of marriage and childbirth.

Poseidon controlled the oceans. His horse-drawn chariot and trident made him instantly recognisable as the god of the sea. Poseidon was also god of horses and earthquakes and is believed to have given the first horse to humans.

Zeus

Zeus's other brother, Hades, was the ruler of the dead and god of the underworld. Greeks believed that when they died their souls would be taken to Hades. Hades had a magic helmet that made the wearer invisible. It was while wearing this helmet that he was able to steal Persephone, daughter of Demeter, and trick her into marrying him.

Gods of city and countryside

Each Greek city was protected by a patron god. The only god who did not have a city to protect or represent was Ares. The god of war was unpopular and mistrusted because of his violent and brutal nature. Ares was unreliable and cowardly in spite of his love of war.

Athena, goddess of wisdom, was the patron goddess of the capital city, Athens. Athena disliked war but she represented courage and victory. It is thought that Athena inspired Odysseus to create the Trojan horse. Despite her skill and intelligence Athena could be jealous and (like all of the gods) unpredictable – perhaps this is why she turned Arachne into a spider after she challenged Athena to a weaving competition.

Athena

Hades

In the countryside, the most important goddess was Demeter, goddess of agriculture. Greek farmers believed that she provided the harvests and taught humans how to farm. As Zeus's sister, Demeter was able to strike a deal with Hades after he stole her daughter, Persephone. Zeus ruled that Persephone should spend two thirds of the year with her husband in the underworld and one-third of the year with her mother. When Persephone is with Hades, Demeter is angry and unhappy, so nothing grows. When Persephone returns to Demeter it is spring again.

Along with Demeter, Dionysus – god of wine and song – was believed to help or hinder the crops and, when pleased, would provide juicy grapes and ripened olives. However, Dionysus was unpredictable and sometimes violent. The half human son of Zeus would often punish those who forgot to worship him.

In the forests and mountains, Artemis, twin sister of Apollo, protected all wild things as goddess of hunting. Artemis was kind and gentle; she is sometimes referred to as goddess of the moon and she was a protector of young girls.

Gods of skill and knowledge
The Greeks believed that the gods possessed different kinds of knowledge and powers that they might choose to share with humans.

Zeus's son, Apollo, carried a golden bow and arrow. The Greeks believed that the god of the Sun used these to shoot rays of sunlight and knowledge at Earth. Apollo shared his skill and knowledge of healing by teaching his son, Asclepius, god of medicine. Like his twin sister, Artemis, Apollo was a protector of the young and took care of young boys.

Hermes was a clever, cunning and quick-witted god. He made Apollo's musical lyre and became a protector of travellers. Because he was swift in his winged shoes and hat, Hermes was the messenger of the gods. It was also thought that Hermes guided the souls of the dead to Hades, across the river Styx.

Apollo and Artemis

Technical knowledge was provided by Hephaestus, god of fire and protector of metal workers. He was a skilled metal worker himself and made many things for the gods, including the golden throne of Zeus and the arrows of Apollo and Artemis. Hephaestus was a powerful god and, despite being ugly, lame and deformed, was married to Aphrodite – most beautiful of all the goddesses and winner of the prized golden apple. Aphrodite was the goddess of love and beauty; she was feminine and soft. The magic girdle that she wore made everyone desire her. Aphrodite is thought to have hated her husband and loved Ares, who was the father of her son Eros.

Greek Gods and Goddesses

Name of god/goddess	Also known as: (god/goddess of...)	Characteristics (personality and appearance)	Relationship with other gods	Other information

Name of god/goddess	Also known as: (god/goddess of...)	Characteristics (personality and appearance)	Relationship with other gods	Other information
Aphrodite	Goddess of love and beauty goddess	Soft, feminine, beautiful, loving, powerful	Married to ugly Hephaestus Loved Ares Mother of Eros prize for most beautiful	Wore a magic girdle that made everyone desire her Won the golden apple as the Animal = dove
Apollo	God of the sun, light, purity and healing	Wore a long shirt of panther skin and a laurel wreath	Son of Zeus Twin brother of Artemis Father of Asclepius	Carried a golden bow and quiver
Ares	God of war	Violent and brutal, cruel but cowardly	Son of Zeus and Hera Loved Aphrodite Father of Eros	Animal = dog
Artemis	Goddess of hunting and wild animals; protector of youth	Kind, gentle, pure	Daughter of Zeus Twin sister of Apollo	Animal = deer
Asclepius	God of medicine		Son of Apollo	Animal = snake (medics use his symbol of a snake around a staff) Punished by Zeus for trying to bring a dead patient back to life
Athena	Goddess of wisdom, courage, craft and victory	Clever, talented, jealous	Daughter of Zeus	Patron of city of Athens Excellent weaver (turned Arachne into a spider after she challenged Athena to a weaving competition) Animal = heifer
Demeter	Goddess of agriculture and harvest		Zeus's sister	Farmers prayed to her for good crops Animal = pig

Sheet C (continued)

Writing across the Curriculum

Name of god/goddess	Also known as: (god/goddess of...)	Characteristics (personality and appearance)	Relationship with other gods	Other information
Dionysus	God of wine and song	Unpredictable, violent	Son of Zeus (mother = mortal human)	Punished those who forgot to worship him Animal = bull
Eros	God of love	Young boy/cherub	Son of Aphrodite and Ares	Carried bow and arrow; when people were hit by his arrow they fell in love
Hades	Ruler of the dead; god of the underworld		Zeus's brother	Had a helmet that made the wearer invisible Stole Demeter's daughter (Persephone) and tricked her into marrying him
Hephaestus	God of fire; protector of metal workers	Lame and deformed but powerful	Married to Aphrodite	Made the golden throne of Zeus
Hera	Goddess of marriage and childbirth	Beautiful, clever, jealous of Zeus's lovers	Zeus's wife (and sister?)	Loved and hated Zeus at the same time Animals = cow and peacock
Hermes	Messenger of the gods Protector of travellers	Swift, cunning, quick-minded	Son of Zeus Friend of Apollo	Made Apollo's lyre Wore winged shoes and hat Guided souls to Hades across the river Styx
Poseidon	God of the sea, horse and earthquakes	Bearded, strong, strict	Zeus' brother	Rode in a horse-drawn chariot Carried a trident Animals = horse and bull
Zeus	Ruler of the gods; god of the sky and thunder	Sense of justice (punished wrong and rewarded right); loved women	See other gods	Ruler of Mount Olympus; sat on golden throne Animal = bull

Unit 2

Lesson focus

Science Unit 5B – Life cycles

Overall aim

To write an explanation/description of the life cycle of a flowering plant, using pictorial notes as a prompt.

Science emphasis

By the end of this unit, the children should be able to describe the processes of pollination, fertilisation, seed dispersal and germination.

Literacy links

Year 5, Term 1: T23, T26; Term 2: T20, T21

About this unit

Prior to commencing this unit, the children should be familiar with the different parts of a plant and the jobs that they do. They should have a simple understanding of what plants need and should know the seven life processes. It would be helpful if they had an understanding of other life cycles, such as of the frog, butterfly and human, and are beginning to use scientific vocabulary when talking about the life cycle of plants.

In terms of note making, the children should understand the need for expressing things in their own words and know that different note making strategies can be used for different purposes. They should also recognise the features of explanation and description writing.
This unit should be taught in conjunction with science lessons and is suited to work within the literacy hour or as part of timetabled science lessons. This method of note making provides excellent opportunities for assessment; by looking at children's notes you can see clearly whether or not they have grasped the scientific concept they are exploring.

Switching on

Learning objective

■ To make notes using picture symbols.

Resources

■ Sheets A and B (pages 132 and 133)

What to do

This is a fun session! Tell the children that you are going to look at a new way of making notes. Explain that this note making technique is particularly useful for explanations and instructions. Tell them that they will eventually use this method of note making to help them write their own explanation of the plant life cycle.

Explain that with these notes, no words will be used. This will probably puzzle them, so ask them what other ways they can think of for communicating ideas instead of using

words. Say that they will be making notes using pictures (or symbols) – it doesn't matter if they think they can't draw because their notes only need to make sense to them; they do not need to be understood by anyone else.

Provide the children with copies of Sheet A and read the text with them. Say that you want them to rewrite the text in pictures or symbols. Tell them they must be sure that they will know at a later date what the picture they have drawn represents. So, for example, to show a young puppy, they could draw a picture of a puppy (even a matchstick one would be fine) and for four small meals they might draw four small dog bowls. Ask for a few volunteers to do their picture notes onto OHTs to look at later. While the children make their notes move around the groups, giving support and encouragement as needed.

When they have finished, collect the copies of Sheet A. Before asking the children to share their notes, show them some that you have made. You could have drawn your own or you could use Sheet B (fold back the part of the sheet that explains what the pictures refer to). Tell them the pieces of information you can recall from Sheet A, using the notes on Sheet B as a prompt. Do the children think the pictures would be useful as notes or can they suggest better pictures?

Plenary

Ask volunteers to share their notes and compare the similarities/differences.

Revving up

Learning objectives

■ To begin to understand the processes within a flowering plant's life cycle.
■ To make notes using picture symbols.

Resources

■ Sheet C (page 134)
■ The notes from the last session

What to do

Begin the session by getting the children to look at their notes from the last session. Can they remember what their notes mean? Ask one or two volunteers to explain what a new dog owner should know. Afterwards, reread the original text (Sheet A) and evaluate the success of the children's notes (this should be quite high). Explain that you are now going to start using this method of note making for science.

Ask the children to tell you what they know about the flowering plant life cycle and record their ideas on the board or flip chart, drawing out scientific vocabulary. Focus on the processes within the life cycle.

Display an enlarged version of Sheet C. Read the explanations of germination and pollination (you may wish to use texts from books you use in school instead). Discuss this with the children to make sure they understand the content. Tell them that you want them to be able to explain each process on the sheet in picture note form. Explain that you will take away the text in a few minutes. (Less able children could be asked to concentrate on only one of the processes.)

After a few minutes remove the text and give the children some more time to complete their notes. When they have had sufficient time put the children into pairs. Ask them to take it in turns to explain/describe a process before joining with another pair to share and evaluate their notes and reminders.

Plenary

At the end of the session reread the original text (Sheet C), asking children to put a tick by each piece of information they remembered or represented in their notes. Discuss the children's success and confidence. Are they surprised by the effectiveness of this type of note making?

Taking off

Learning objectives

■ To develop knowledge and understanding of the processes in a flowering plant's life cycle.

■ To make notes using picture symbols.

Resources

■ Sheets D and E (pages 135 and 136)

What to do

Share an enlarged version of Sheet D (each child will also need their own copy to make notes from). Identify each stage in the life cycle. Follow the text from different starting points so that the children can see the cyclical nature of the stages. Tell them that in the next session they will be writing their own explanation/description of the life cycle (perhaps as a revision guide for Year 6) and that they will be using their picture notes from this session. Explain that they need to remember the details of each stage/process as well as the sequence.

Ask the children to make picture notes for Sheet D. If you wish, Sheet E can be used as a format for their notes. As they are working, spend time supporting the children and guiding them towards the 'key' pieces of information.

Plenary

End the session by collecting in the texts and asking the children to work in pairs to talk through their notes – this talking and explaining will help the children to remember more easily in the next session, which should be carried out after a space of time (after lunch or the next day).

Flying solo

Learning objective

■ To be able to write an explanation of a flowering plant's life cycle using notes.

Resources

■ Sheet F (page 137)

■ Children's notes from the last session

What to do

Tell the children that today they will be using their notes about the plant life cycle to write an explanation.

Show them the picture notes for one process (Sheet F). Say that you are going to show them how to turn these pictorial notes into a written explanation of the process.

The children should think that you are really making it up as you go along. The idea is that you show them how to write while explaining your thinking at the same time. The bold print is what you actually write and the italics can be used as a script of what to say out loud as if to yourself.

You only need to model one of the processes but notes are provided for both:

Right, I'm going to use the picture notes to write an explanation of germination/pollination. (Choose one and write the title.)

Germination

Well, the picture shows a seed under the soil with rain, sunshine and a nose...? Oh yes, we breathe air; the nose represents the air... **The seed needs the right amount**... *because different plants will need different conditions* ...**of water, warmth and air to start to grow.** *Okay, the next picture shows me how the seed* grows. **Germination** ... I'm using the scientific vocabulary ... **happens when the seed produces a root and a shoot.**

Or

Pollination

I know that this is to do with the transfer of pollen. The picture notes show the pollen going from the stamen to the stigma. The wasp or bee must represent insects and the cloud blowing must be ... the wind? Right, how am I going to put this into sentences? I will start with a general statement. **Pollen from the stamen is transferred onto the sticky stigma of another plant.** *That sounds okay. It can happen in several ways. Ee have learned about two ways. So I need to describe these ... new sentence.* **The pollen may** ... *this shows possibilities...* **be blown by the wind** ... **or**... *to show an alternative* ...**it might be carried on the bodies of insects** ... *why would insects carry pollen? Ah yes,* **as they move from flower to flower in search of nectar.**

Reread the writing out loud. Have you included all the relevant information? Is there anything that the children think should be included or changed?

Now ask the children to use their notes in the same way to write their explanation. Remind them that as long as the processes are in the correct order it doesn't matter which process they start with because the life cycle is a continuous process. Work with a group to target intervention and support where it is needed.

Ask the children to share what they have written with a partner and when they are satisfied that their explanations are correct, they can make them into a poster with pictures and writing.

Plenary

Set up mini displays of the children's posters. Lay them on the table in groups and allow the children a few minutes to move around the class and look at each other's. Ask the children to tell you what made the best ones the most effective. Did the posters contain the same key information? Ask the children to review what they have learned (about literacy and/or science) and discuss the effectiveness of picture notes – has this method helped them to develop their understanding?

How to look after your dog
(Information for new dog owners)

A young dog, or puppy, needs four small meals a day to help it grow and develop. An older dog only needs two meals a day in order to keep its strength up. When feeding your dog, make sure that you give it a balanced diet. Each meal should include a mixture of meat and biscuits. You will also need to give your dog a clean bowl of fresh water every day.

Dogs can be given a large bone to gnaw on as these help their teeth to stay strong and clean. Dogs should not be given small bones to chew because they might splinter. These splinters might get stuck in the dog's throat which could be very dangerous.

You should brush and comb your dog every day to keep its coat clean and shiny. Give your pet a blanket to sleep on and make sure that it gets plenty of exercise – you will need a collar and lead and should take your dog for a walk every day.

Do not let the children see this part – these notes give you information about each picture.

1. Puppies = 4 meals a day
   Older dogs = 2 meals
   Fresh water every day
   Biscuits + meat mix

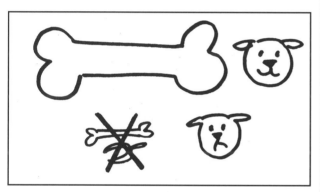

2. Big bones = good for teeth
   Small bones can splinter – choking

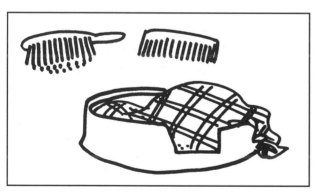

3. Brush and comb every day
   Need blanket and basket

4. Need collar and lead
   Walk every day

Flowering plants

Germination

Germination occurs when seeds start to grow; they produce a root and a shoot. Seeds need the right amount of warmth, air and moisture to germinate. They do not necessarily need soil (seeds will germinate in cotton wool or on tissue paper, for example) and, although plants need light to grow healthily, seeds do not need light to germinate.

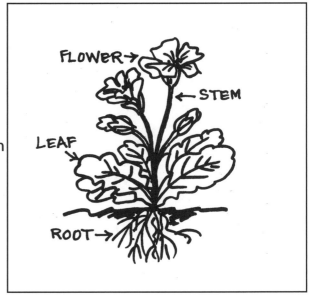

Pollination

Pollination is important for flowering plant reproduction. Pollination occurs when pollen from the stamen of one plant is transferred onto the sticky stigma of another plant. Pollination can be carried out by insects or by the wind.

Pollination by insects:
Insects are attracted to the flowers by the scent and coloured petals. The insects look for nectar and get covered in pollen. When they move to another plant they carry the pollen with them and transfer it to the stigma, which is sticky.

Pollination by the wind:
If plants are pollinated by the wind they usually have longer stamens. These long stamens are blown about by the wind, which releases the pollen. The pollen is then blown onto the stigma of another plant.

Sheet D

Seed production
The flower dies and leaves behind a fruit. The fruit contains seeds (the fruit is actually a fertilised ovule).

Seed dispersal
The seed must be carried away from the parent plant to reduce competition for space, light and nutrients. Seeds can be dispersed in three ways:

- By wind   The fruits and seeds are light so they get blown by the wind.
- By animals   The fruits are juicy or sticky so either they get eaten by the animals who then excrete the seeds, or they stick to the animals' fur and are carried away.
- By explosion The fruit pod dries up and splits open. This sends the seeds shooting out.

Germination
The seed begins to grow into a new plant because it has the right amount of air, moisture and warmth.

Plant growth
The seedling grows into a larger plant.

Flower formation
Flowers contain the reproductive organs of the plant. The flower contains the pollen and ovule which will eventually make seeds if they are fertilised. The flowers will attract insects and birds.

Pollination
Pollen from the stamen is transferred to another plant where it is caught by the sticky stigma. Pollination can happen in two ways:

- By wind   The long stamens are blown about in the wind and pollen is carried to the stigma.
- By insects   The insect is attracted by the flower's scent and colour. While looking for nectar the insect becomes covered in pollen. When the insect moves on to another flower it carries the pollen with it and the pollen sticks to the stigma.

Fertilisation
After pollination the pollen reaches the ovary where it joins with the ovule. When the pollen and ovule join, the ovule is fertilised and can now produce more seeds.

The Life Cycle of a Flowering Plant

Sheet F

Germination

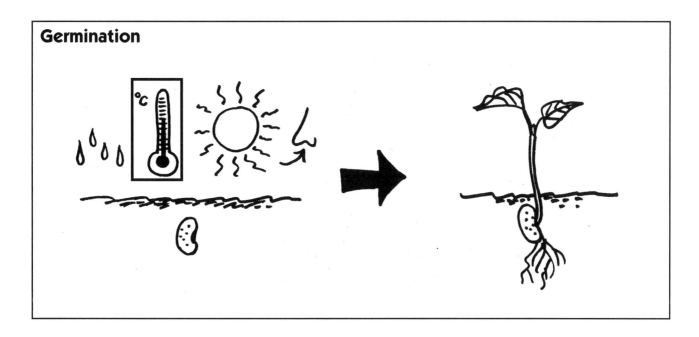

Pollination